BALLATER GOLF CLUB

——— 1892~1992 ———

'If you would see a perfect picture postcard stretch of Scotland take the road from Braemar to Ballater any afternoon when the sun is shining. All the graciousness, all the gentleness, all the sweetness and the prettiness which is denied the mountain pass from Perth has taken root in the valley of the Dee. Here on fine days the Highlands wear a perpetual smile.'

H.V. Morton: In Search of Scotland.

BALLATER GOLF CLUB

—— *1892~1992* ——

Peter MacPhee

PICTURE CREDITS

Jim Henderson LMPA — pp. 65, 75
Aberdeen Journals — pp. 79, 129
Clive W. Couch — pp. 92, 118
DuCam Marketing (UK) Ltd — p. 29
George Washington Wilson Collection — p. 12
© Crown copyright 1992/MOD reproduced with
the permission of the Controller of the HMSO
— Front endpaper

Ab44426
150636

Front endpaper: The Golf Course from 10,000 feet.
Back endpaper: The Report and Accounts for 1906.

First published in Great Britain in 1992

ISBN 0 9518793 0 8

Designed by Kate MacPhee

Typeset, from the Author's keystrokes, by Servis Filmsetting, Manchester
Printed in Great Britain by The Bath Press

Contents

Foreword

BY CAPTAIN A.A.C. FARQUHARSON OF INVERCAULD, M.C.

Of the many gifts which Scotland can claim to have given the world in the sphere of sport surely the game of golf must rank foremost. The origins of the game are of great antiquity. Even the Romans had a shot at it playing a game they called 'paganica' with a crooked stick and a ball stuffed with feathers. But the Scots then took it over and by the mid 15th century they had established it as a national sport, so much so that several Acts of Parliament had to be passed forbidding it in the interests of archery. However a century later it came into its own when in 1553 the Bishop of St Andrews ratified the rights of the community to the Links 'for the playing of Golfe'. Throughout the next three centuries it remained virtually confined to Scotland, thereafter being gradually exported to other parts of the world until today there is scarcely a country to be found without a golf course.

Golf is a game in the playing of which youth and age can combine; to be enjoyed in peaceful and picturesque surroundings, yet a test of both skill and character. Golf carries with it in its traditions and in its play the pride of Scotland. It is therefore a privilege and a pleasure to have the opportunity through this foreword of reaffirming the ongoing harmonious and close links between Invercauld and my family and the Ballater Golf Club on the occasion of the celebration of their centenary, and of wishing the Club and its members continuing success and prosperity through the next hundred years.

November 1991

6

Captain A.A.C. Farquharson of Invercauld, M.C.

Author's Note and Acknowledgements

The Royal and Ancient Golf Club of St Andrews has not yet invited the Ballater Golf Club to host the Open Championship, the Amateur Championships, or the Walker Cup. (In any case the Manager assures me that the course is fully booked for the Centenary year!) For the historian this has a distinct disadvantage; there can be no padding out with accounts of the heroic golfing deeds and fairway progress of the great and famous—apart, that is, from Braid and Vardon who played the Ballater course in 1906. This being so, the historian, having only the slightest acquaintance with Ballater, (a round in 1947 and another in 1961), until recent residence in retirement, has had to draw heavily on Club records, local newspapers, Libraries, the memories of Ballater folk of all ages and occupations, and of other friends of Ballater living elsewhere. It's been a rich haul!

The Club records in the form of minutes of Council meetings exist from day one and they have been read and re-read. In bygone days, particularly in the thirties, forties, and fifties, competition books were meticulously maintained and they included press cuttings. But in recent years there is evidence of a waning interest—hence the occasional blanks in the scores recorded in the text.

Many members have contributed (some without knowing it) as a result of direct interrogation or casual conversation on the golf course, in the bar, or at the street corner. Past Captains and Senior members with long memories have been of great assistance, in particular Matt and Rose Michie, Norman Thain, Tom Forbes, and Harry Wright.

I would also like to thank Dr Sheila Sedgwick for her helpful information about James R. Middleton.

8

In the course of finding out about the Ballater Golf Club I have amassed a great deal of information about people and past events which are not strictly related to the subject in hand. Some of this has crept into the text because I found it interesting. I hope that interest is shared by the reader.

Bert Ingram, the Club Manager has been of tremendous assistance. I hate to think of the number of times he must have seen me approaching across the car park and wished he could be elsewhere! Many thanks, Bert.

I also received much valuable information from Alan Gibb, from Anne Greig, daughter of John Keiller Greig, from Henry Jebb, grandson of H.S.F. Jebb, and from Dr Dudley Yarrow, and Freddie Griffith-Jones, grandsons of Fred Yarrow. Thanks also to Rhod McEwen who helped me track down Grant Speath, and Nigel Franks who provided the clue which led me to the Ternemny Farm Ogilvies.

I spent many interesting hours in the Aberdeen Central Reference Library, and the Woodside Library. Also in the Queen Mother Library, and the Special Collections Archives at the University of Aberdeen. At the Kincardine and Deeside District Council offices in Stonehaven I was given access to the Minutes of the Ballater Town Council meetings. In all these patience and courtesy were shown and I am very grateful.

Thanks also to Graham MacDonald of the Ballater Field Centre for his nature notes and for reminding me that there is more to life than just walking around the fringes of a golf course with ones head down looking for a little white ball! (But not a lot!)

Colin Farquharson, of *Aberdeen Journals*, has as usual been very helpful and I have drawn heavily on the sports columns of his pages in the *Press and Journal* and the *Evening Express*. I have also used material from the *Deeside Piper* and John Campbell's lovely piece about Dick Walker (Appendix Three) comes from *The Sunday Telegraph*.

Finally, thanks Kate.

Introduction

BALLATER (POPULATION 1200, ELEVATION 183m)

Ballater stands between the north bank of the river Dee and Craigendarroch (rocky hill of the oak wood), in the Kincardine and Deeside District of the Grampian Region of Scotland. The City of Aberdeen lies 42 miles to the east between the mouths of the rivers Dee and Don. To the west of Ballater the road follows the course of the Dee past Balmoral Castle to Braemar. Here the river continues westward to its source, while the road turns south to the Cairnwell Ski slopes, and on to Blairgowrie and Perth.

The Rev. James R. Middleton, a Founder Member of the Golf Club, in an article in the *Deeside Field*, 1922, gave some key dates in the development of Ballater. The town arose, he wrote, from the demand for accommodation due to the fame of the Wells of Pannanich in the latter half of the 18th century. Queen Victoria's arrival at Balmoral in 1848 gave a new attraction to the district and by 1861 the population was 362. The extension of the railway from Aboyne to Ballater in 1866 opened the way for visitors and enabled the town to become a popular summer resort. The population grew rapidly rising to 1256 in 1901. Since then it has stabilised at about 1200 although it grows to 3000 plus during the holiday season.

Much of the surrounding land is in private ownership. The largest estate is Invercauld, the greater part of which lies to the west of Ballater stretching along the line of the north side of the Dee beyond Balmoral which is owned by Her Majesty the Queen, and Abergeldie owned by the Gordon family. Across the Dee to the south-west is the Glen Muick estate and to the south-east, Glen Tanar.

When the Golf Club was formed in 1892 permission to create a course had to be obtained from the Laird of Invercauld with the agreement of the tenant farmer, Alexander Mitchell of Sluievannachie, a farm

10

immediately to the west of the town on the north side of the river. Several holes, the 5th, 6th, and the 13th in particular, run close to the river, and a hook or a pull from the 13th tee will surely find water. The course is surrounded by hills.

To the north, and closest of all the hills is Craigendarroch (402m)—the plum pudding hill of our schooldays—behind which, but hidden from view from the course, is Morven (872m). To the right of Craigendarroch there is a view of Culblean Hill (477m), site of a famous battle in 1335. To the east there is the valley of the Dee and the road to Aberdeen. To the south-east there is the Pannanich Hill (601m) on the lower slopes of which are the Wells where, having sampled the water, 'the auld seem young and frisky', according to the poet, Dr John Ogilvie.

Craig Vallach (609m) lies to the south guarding the entrance to Glen Muick whose river flows from Loch Muick and runs downstream (at one point over a spectacular waterfall) some eight miles before joining the Dee west of the town.

Looking south-west the Coyles of Muick (601m) can be seen and behind them the tip of Lochnagar (1111m)—of 'The Old Man of . . .' fame. Lochnagar can be seen from the more easterly points on the course, and more clearly, perhaps, from the upstairs Bar in the Club-house. To the west there is Creag Liath (458m), Tom an Lagain (423m), and Creag Phiobaidh (449m). Finally, to the north-west there is Carn Dearg (594m) and to its right the glen through which the river Gairn flows southwards joining the Dee a mile or so short of the town.

Ballater has much to offer the visitor. Apart from the Golf there is, Bowls, Tennis, or Putting (on a huge green)—all close to the Clubhouse and the pro's shop. In the surrounding hills there are many walks, and climbs. There is, of course, fishing and shooting and for those inclined upwards there is gliding strip beyond Dinnet to the east of Ballater. Local fishermen have an angling club with permission from the Inver-cauld Estate to use Loch Vrotachan located behind the Cairnwell ski slopes. Permits may be obtained from the 'Rod and Tackle' store in Bridge Street.

During the Victoria Week in August and at other times during the tourist season there is a great deal of indoor and outdoor entertainment organised by the community. The Tourist Board office is in the Albert Hall opposite the old Railway Station.

A mile to the north the western slopes of Craigendarroch have been developed so that the former smallish hotel is now a 50 bedroom 4-star hotel with a Country Club and Time Ownership lodges.

The folk who live in or around Ballater, whether native, incomer, or welcome visitor mostly all think that the town and its surrounds are very, very special.

11

ONE

Friday, 5th August, 1892

The weather forecast was for south-westerly to westerly breezes; dull; rainy. The maximum temperature was to be 61°F. Sports news that morning included this from the *Aberdeen Journal*:

Braemar. The fishing here, as a natural result of the droughty, dry weather has of late fallen off greatly, although occasional good takes are reported. On Wednesday a gentleman from The Invercauld Arms ('McGregor's') landed no fewer than nine salmon from 6 to 12 lbs each on the Invercauld private water.

In August 1892 the population of Ballater and its surrounds (i.e. the Parishes of Glen Gairn, Glenmuick, and Tullich) was about 2300. The Registrar was John Riach and Miss Farquharson ran the Post Office. The Town Councillors were W. Connon, W. Deans (of the Temperance Hotel), C. Ferrier, J. Mitchell, J. Anderson, and R. Davidson one of five Bank Agents. (Today Ballater has three Banks. At times during the last 100 years the town has had five Shoe shops—nowadays there is one.)

There were two Doctors—Mitchell and Cran. The Tenant Proprietor of the main Hotel and its farm, the Invercauld, was J. McGregor.

It was one of the Bank Agents, *John Simpson*, who had invited seven men to meet him that morning in his quarters above the Union Bank in Bridge Street to discuss the formation of a Golf Club. John Simpson was also the Burgh Council Treasurer and Collector. The men invited to the meeting were:

James Robert Middleton, M.A. Born Glenmuick Manse, Ballater, 23rd January, 1860. M.A.(Aberdeen) 1881. He was ordained in August 1884 and took over at Glenmuick on the death of his father, John Middleton, in 1884.

James Middleton was a cultured man, very active in local affairs. He

13

LEFT *Craigendarroch from a point between the present 7th and 16th fairway with Darroch Learg and Oakhall to the left.* c. *1890.*

drafted various addresses on behalf of the village, e.g. on the deaths of Queen Victoria and Edward VII. Poor health led to his retirement in 1928. He died in 1934 and was buried in Glenmuick. His widow, Elizabeth Davidson Grant Wilson died in 1948. His daughter, Helen, died in Surrey in 1990 at the age of 92.

John Lawson, M.A. Session Clerk, Schoolteacher, and Junior Magistrate.

John Brebner, School Board Chairman and Magistrate.

William Gordon Mitchell, M.A. M.D. M.B. C.M. 1895 Edinburgh University. Medical Officer of Health, Glenmuick, Tullich, and Glen Gairn. Surg. Lt. 5th V.B. Gordon Highlanders. Cambridge Cottage, Ballater.

John McGregor. Tenant of The Invercauld Arms Hotel and farm.

Alexander Mitchell. Tenant farmer of Sluievannachie and horse hirer. Mitchell was born in 1838 and died in 1922. His wife, Isabella Ballantyne died in 1938 also aged 84.

William Barnett. Provost, Chief Magistrate, and General Merchant with a shop in Bridge Street.

Some of these men must have known something about golf; perhaps they had played over the course at Aboyne (founded 1883), or at Royal Aberdeen (1780). Other Clubs in the area older than Ballater are Oldmeldrum (1885), Peterhead (1841), and Fraserborough (1881). It is more than likely though that James Middleton and John Lawson had been exposed to golf when they were students at Aberdeen University.

William Barnett

John Brebner

Likewise it is probable that Dr Mitchell enjoyed the game when attending Edinburgh University.

Recent research has revealed that a few golf holes were prepared on the ground below the Pannanich Wells Hotel and were brought into use around 1910. They could not have played a part in the introduction of golf to Ballater and they are not used nowadays.

*　　　　*　　　　*

The History of the Club is inscribed in the Minutes of the many Council and General meetings held over the last hundred years. The proceedings of these meetings were faithfully hand written into books by the Secretaries until 1959 when the typewriter took over to be followed recently by the word processor.

Mr Norman D.F. Tosh, a schoolteacher, who was a member, made extracts from the minutes up to December 1968 when he died suddenly on the course. His daughter subsequently gave his notebooks to the Club and they have been of assistance.

Union Bank House,
Ballater.
5th August, 1892

A meeting called by John Simpson, Union Bank, Ballater was held here this morning for the purpose of forming a Golf Club. The gentlemen invited to be present were Messrs John Brebner, William Barnett, John Lawson, Alexander Mitchell, Dr W.G. Mitchell, John McGregor, and Rev. James R. Middleton.

Present—Messrs Brebner, Barnett, Mitchell, McGregor, and Mr Middleton, Dr Mitchell and Mr Lawson being unavoidably absent but agreed to act as Councillors if wished. Mr Simpson read the following letter from Mr Foggo.

1st August 1892
Invercauld Office,
Ballater,
Aberdeenshire.

Dear Sir,

Referring to your letter of 5th ulto, there will be no objection to the waste lands by the riverside at Sluievannachie being used for golf provided the Tenant's crops are not injured by parties going to and from the golf course when it is formed and used. Mr Heaven, the Tenant of Monaltrie does not object as far as he is concerned.

R.G. Foggo

Mr Mitchell, Sluievannachie, who was present said he had no objection to the land in question being used as a golf course—free of charge.

Name. The name of the club shall be the Ballater Golf Club.

15

BALLATER GOLF CLUB.

The following are the conditions on which Players are admitte
to the Green:—

Member's Entrance Fee,	. .	**10s.**
Do. **Annual Subscription,**		**5s.**
Visitors for the Season,	. .	**10s.**
Do. for One Month,	. .	**5s.**
Do. for One Week,	. .	**2s. 6d.**
Do. for One Day,	. . .	**1s.**

Tickets may be had on applying to Mr. WILLIAM BARNET
Merchant, Ballater.

Ticket-holders will be good enough to show their Tickets to th
Green-keeper when asked to do so.

Players, in passing to or from the Course, are requested to kee
to the path and not trespass on the adjoining fields.

Dogs are not allowed on to the Course.

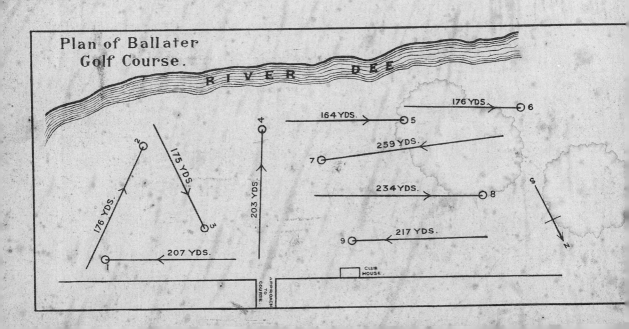

Plan of Ballater Golf Course.

Patron. A.H. Farquharson of Invercauld was unanimously proposed. Mr Simpson was instructed to write to Mr Farquharson and ask if he will allow his name to be put down as such.

Captain. John Simpson, Union Bank, was appointed Captain for the current year.

Councillors. The following gentlemen agreed to act as Councillors. Messrs Brebner, Barnett, Mitchell, Rev. Mr Middleton, Dr Mitchell, and Mr Lawson.

Secretary. Mr John McGregor.

Entrance money on admission shall be 10/- and the *Annual subscription* shall be 2/6 payable in advance to the Secretary.

Temporary residenters who become members of the Club to have the privilege of allowing members of the family (ladies and boys under 16) to play on paying a fee of 2/6 for the summer months.

Non-members 2/6 a week. *Life members* by paying Five Pounds.

Agreed to adopt the Rules of the Aberdeen Golf Club. Golfers not to be allowed to take dogs to the golf course.

The Secretary was instructed to order a mower.

Signed   John Simpson   Captain

In April 1893 the Committee agreed that 'all games be played under the St Andrews Rules of the game of golf'. At the same meeting it was thought desirable to erect a clubhouse and, in view of the heavy outlay, it was decided to find out from Mr Foggo, if Mr Farquharson would assist the Club by supplying the timber free of charge.

Mr Mitchell continued to give the land free of charge and in 1895 the Committee decided to make Mrs Mitchell a present of a portable greenhouse.

In April 1900 John Simpson wrote to the Club intimating his resignation as Captain but Alex Mitchell opposed this pointing out that Simpson was 'one of the gentlemen to whom he had originally given permission to use the grounds as a golf course and it was essential that he continue as Captain'. Simpson agreed to do so but two years later in May 1902 his resignation as Captain was accepted and James Grant became the second Ballater Golf Club Captain.

TWO

Sluievannachie Farm

In 1892 the land to the west of Ballater on the north side of the Dee was owned by the Estate of Invercauld & Monaltrie. The Tenant farmer of Sluievannachie, the flattish area close to the town, was Alexander Mitchell ('Sluie' Mitchell) and it was this ground that was viewed with particular interest by those who saw it as a natural arena for a golf course. The first nine hole course was laid out on waste land beyond the cultivated area of Sluievannachie farm. Golfers would have to cross the cropped land to reach the course. Alex Mitchell, a member of the Golf Club Council, granted the newly formed Club free use of this area.

The first mention of the course being extended was at a meeting of the Greens Committee on 22nd June 1903 when:

> It was agreed to ask Archie Simpson of Royal Aberdeen [1780] and James Donaldson of Deeside Golf Club [1903] to give an exhibition match in July ... Mr Simpson to be asked to advise the Club as to lengthening the course.

Archie Simpson played in the Open Championship a number of times. In 1885 he was second. In 1890 he was again second together with Willie Fernie of Troon, three shots behind John Ball Jnr. of Royal Liverpool. At that time he was playing out of Carnoustie but moved to Aberdeen, (after a spell at Prestwick), 'as professional and greens superintendant' in 1895 and continued playing in the Open until 1906. He finished in the first ten on a number of occasions. According to the Royal Aberdeen golf historian 'he was a gifted and seemingly likeable character [who] popularised the game through frequent exhibitions'. He left the Aberdeen club in 1912 when he emigrated to the States. 'A glorious driver with a glorious swing.'

However at a meeting of the Committee a week later it was apparent that the plans had gone awry because 'letters were read from Messrs

18

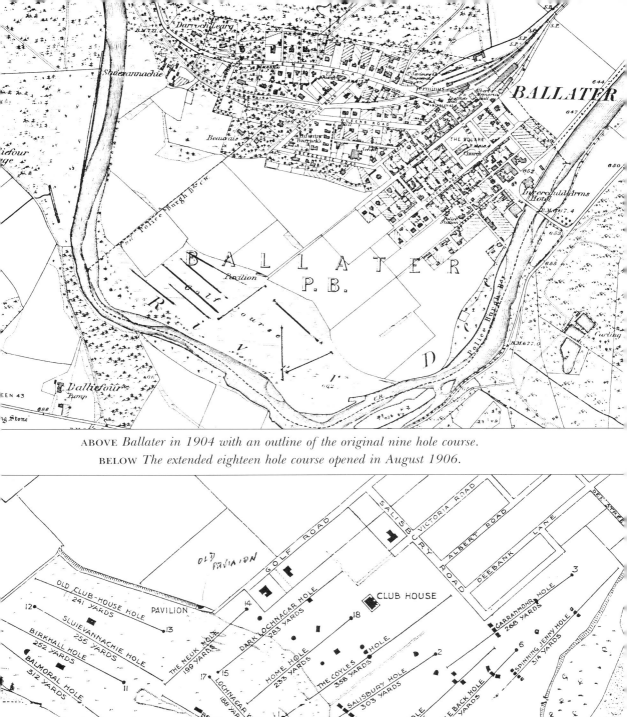

ABOVE *Ballater in 1904 with an outline of the original nine hole course.*
BELOW *The extended eighteen hole course opened in August 1906.*

Simpson and Donaldson relative to the proposed exhibition match and it was agreed that on account of the nature of the replies the offers be not accepted.' There is nothing in the records to tell us what was said in the replies but it was likely about remuneration.

Almost a year went by before the matter was raised again. A Special Meeting of the Club was called for 11th May, 1904 to consider the question of the extension of the course to 18 holes. Messrs W. Willox, W. Beekie, and Tom Lambert (Secretary) were appointed the Golf Course Extension Committee (GCEC) and authorised to make arrangements for an expert to inspect the ground. Alex Mitchell indicated that he was prepared to make land available provided he was compensated.

During the next ten months many meetings were held, and there was a great deal of acrimonious correspondence before all the difficulties had been ironed out.

Towards the end of May 1904 the GCEC decided to write to Mr Smith, the Invercauld Estate Factor enclosing a sketch of the proposed golf course asking the terms on which the course could be leased, with power to sub-let the grazing ... 'and would he please inform Mr Mitchell'. During the next few months discussions with the Factor continued; the first sign of difficulty coming when the GCEC met Mr Mitchell on 4th October in order to hear what compensation he was seeking. The terms were considered harsh and Mr Tosh in transcribing the Minutes adds 'the Committee must have listened to this in grim silence!'. The following day the GCEC informed Mr Mitchell that they had decided to procure the services of an expert to advise on compensation.

The Secretary wrote to James Farquhar, Auctioneer and Valuator, Old Echt, Aberdeenshire who responded that he was seeking information from Mr Mitchell and would arrive in Ballater on Tuesday 29th October at 11.48 a.m., [aboard a train which alas! no longer has a track on which to run]. The Committee were not pleased with Mr Farquhar's initial response as he appeared to be offering to arbitrate.

The Secretary wrote to the Valuator asking him to keep to his original instructions, continuing:

> that the Golf Club had no intention of submitting the case between them and Mr Mitchell to mutual arbitrament and all they wish of Mr Farquhar is his professional estimate of the probable value per acre of a crop on the two lea fields so as to enable the Committee to offer Mr Mitchell fair compensation, the case being simply this ... Mr Mitchell says he is entitled to a grain crop on the two fields and the Committee wish it left in grass and furthermore would he please forward his report and account by 23rd January.

Mr Farquhar replied that he quite understood the position regarding arbitrament and that the Committee would have his report and estimate on Monday 24th, adding 'you are quite at liberty to withdraw my commission at any time'.

The report, which is somewhat technical, arrived as promised and the GCE Committee met to consider it. They wasted little time in deciding to pay no attention to it whatever! Instead they decided, 'to accept the valuation of two arbiters, one to be named by each party, or of an oversman appointed by such arbiters'.

The Club wrote to Mr Mitchell along these lines outlining what action it would take regarding compensation if he didn't give his approval, and pointing out that in accordance with their agreement the Club had the privilege of playing over the ground until Whit Sunday 1905, and that they didn't consider that he could plough it up without giving a years notice.

This produced a stinging, forthright response from Mr Mitchell whose letter included confirmation of his original demands for compensation and that he was agreeable to get a Valuator to value the dung, labour, rent of land for turnips etc. He continued:

> About arable land on the present course — you seem to think I have no right to plough without giving you one years notice. I say there was no such agreement . . . the ground is mine at present, and unless I get £3 per acre I will plough it . . . I will now give you a little information as you seem to think I was unreasonable. The two lea fields had over two hundred loads of turnips carted on to them and eaten by sheep. The largest field had the manure of six horses for a year carted on as top dressing.
>
> The said manure was from the horses that were driving the wood to the saw-mill. The field in fallow had in 1902 and 1903, 150 loads of Swedish turnips from Knock farm carted and eaten on it . . . As to the Club getting valuation. I am afraid they might get a little surprise as my bills for corn, hay, straw, cake, bran etc . . . will come to over £600 per year. . . . You may not be aware that I arranged with Mr Smith last year for a renewal of my lease from year to year with a year's notice . . . Unless my offer is accepted in five days . . . I will start ploughing up my three lea fields.

The Factor was sent a copy of this letter asking for his opinion. He replied that he was astonished at Mr Mitchell's statement regarding retention of the farm for a further year and suggesting that there must be a mistake as there had never been any such arrangement.

But in the meantime the Club became concerned with Mr Mitchell's response and they decided to bring in the Advocates. The facts, as the Club saw them, were put to Messrs Whincup, Carle and Duthie, Union Street, Aberdeen and Mr D. Hutcheon Duthie wrote to Mr Mitchell. Nevertheless Mr Mitchell wrote as follows to Mr Smith, on 3rd March:

> I don't think the Golf Club and me are likely to come to a settlement, therefore, as promised, I write to let you know as I think of beginning to plough in the beginning of the week. I had a couple of letters from them but have taken no notice as I don't intend to alter in the very least.

21

About the arable land on present course—I gave them liberty to play ... but gave them no right to the ground. They had it for nothing for a number of years, and if I charged them anything, it was for damage to grass. They could not cut whins or broom or alter anything without my permission. I was under no obligation not to plough or do anything I pleased. I can therefore plough the arable land on the course unless I get valuation. They say they have it until May—that is not so, as I was not at the Spring meeting to sanction their getting it for the year, and never signed any agreement whatsoever ...

I certainly don't want to plough the land if I get value for cropping, but otherwise I will do so.

As they only have the arable land up to Golf Road, the upper half of the course belongs to me for another year. . . .

I don't want to trouble you but think it best I should treat you as incoming tenant, you to get a valuation, I to get another, and an oversman mutually chosen if necessary.

I would suggest ... I'll accept this—you could offer them all the grass South of Golf Road at £3 per acre, I to be allowed to pasture it for another year. They to get possession of it at once and lay out any greens etc. they may want. For the present course they to pay £12, I to pasture it for another year. The field after turnips (the clean land) I to crop and they to pay £2 per acre for unexhausted manures. This would be all my claim for manures. They to supply grass seeds for both fields.

This offer is made in its entirety, and if they don't accept I would just go out in the usual way and treat you as my incoming tenant.

I would be obliged by your letting me know by the beginning of the week what arrangement you come to as I would have to start ploughing then.

The Factor sent a copy of this letter to the Club who sent a copy to Mr Duthie, the Advocate, with a letter dated 8th March:

At a meeting of the GCEC. . . . It was decided that I ask you to have everything in readiness for interdicting Mr Alex Mitchell from ploughing up part of the present golf course. There is no special hurry but we should like you to be in readiness so that on receipt of a wire you could obtain an interdict. . . .

The members of the GCEC are: William Willox (Capt), Aboyne Cottage, James Grant, Osborne House, J. Beaton, North of Scotland Bank House, William Beekie, Golf Road, and myself.

We just wish to be prepared for eventualities ... and hope that an interdict is not required.

Mr Duthie was away from the office for a few days and it was not until 14th March that he responded informing the Club that it would be necessary for them to have a Club Meeting to authorise the GCEC to take legal steps to interdict Mr Mitchell in the event his doing anything to injure the present golf course and to authorise them to sue in the name of the Club.

However events now took a course for the better. Mitchell wrote to the Factor setting out new terms and at a meeting of the GCEC on 16th March it was decided not to proceed with Mr Duthie's recommendation. The Secretary wrote to Mr Duthie expressing the thanks of the Committee for the services he had rendered. Mr Mitchell's letter to the Factor, dated 14th March, was conciliatory in tone and, excluding some technicalities, it read:

> I must apologise for not writing you sooner about ground to be taken over for golf course. I measured the ground and there is 17 acres in the lea fields without including Smith Hairdresser's feu, and five acres on the golf course.
>
> I value it at 17 ac: Lea @ £4 per acre = £68. Five acres on Golf course £2.10/- per acre = £12.10/-. Land on course above Golf Road £10. I to get the crop off the fallow and clean land fields and £11 for unexhausted manure on the whole of clean land fields.
>
> The lowest I will accept is £84 in slump [i.e. in one lump] to have no more bother. They would have to pay me £6 at May term for damage to grass up to that time. This is the usual £6.
>
> If this is not satisfactory you can get your valuator and I will get mine and get it valued unexhausted manures and all.
>
> I hear they are to let the grass to Mr Troup [the gardener at Balmoral Castle] for his sheep. I have no objections, but I will hold you responsible for damage done to crops, as they would have to be better fenced . . . to keep out sheep that are only there for a week or so.

Mr Mitchell's letter was good news and at a meeting on 17th March it was agreed that the terms be accepted. They decided to inform the Factor and Mr Mitchell, at the same time telling him that they had not been in touch with the Balmoral Mr Troup—in fact this may have been a confusion with Mr Troup the Ballater butcher who *was* being offered grass for sheep grazing. The Club also decided to write to the Braemar Golf Club [1902] asking the price they had paid for the grass seed they had used and to write similarly to Mr Troup, the Balmoral gardener, and Messrs Smith and Son, Exchange Street, Aberdeen, asking what kind of seed they would recommend for permanent pasture on a golf course.

An agreement was drawn up and signed by Alex Mitchell and the Factor and on 29th March the Secretary writes to the Football Club:

> I am instructed by the Ballater Golf Club to ask your Club to cease play on the land now in possession of the Golf Club and to remove the goal posts.

From time to time the Club draws attention to the fact that Mr Mitchell's horses are grazing on the golf course and asking him to attend to the matter. In 1903, during the earlier years, before the course extension they wrote to Mitchell:

to ask your permission to erect at each of the nine putting Greens 4 poles, about 3½ feet high, one at each corner . . . connected by white covered wire . . . the object being to keep the horses off the putting greens. To be erected every year at the beginning of winter. . . .

*   *   *

In July 1911 the Committee wrote to the Factor asking if it would be possible for the Club to lease an extra piece of land to the north-west of the golf course. The Factor replied:

> Mr Farquharson is quite willing the Golf Club get this ground, but as it is held by Mr Mitchell under lease, he would prefer your Committee arrange direct to rent this from him rather than cause Mr Farquharson to terminate his lease, which I may say he has power to do at Whitsunday next under certain circumstances and I do not think they would find much difficulty in dealing with Mr Mitchell. However should they fail to do so, and wish me to arrange matters, I will be glad to do so on hearing from you.

The Club wrote to Mitchell who replied that he 'was not inclined to give, or rent, the ground . . .' and the Secretary wrote to the Factor asking him to arrange the matter as he had said he would. This was done and in October Dr A.C. Profeit was able to announce to a General Meeting that the additional land was to be leased from the following

Golfers on the extended course — post-1906.

month and that they were approaching J.H. Taylor regarding the new layout. Presumably nothing came of this because a few weeks later William Fernie the Professional at Troon was engaged and he attended a Club meeting where he outlined a plan and it was agreed to proceed.

At the AGM on 1st May 1912 it was stated that the rent for the additional land would be £15 per annum and that Sluie Mitchell was to be paid £20 compensation. The members considered the rent very high and the Secretary was asked to approach the Factor to see if more reasonable terms could be arranged. Mitchell offered to reduce the rent by £2 if the Club left him a piece of the land. There was unanimous disapproval at this and the Committee decided to accept the terms previously offered.

There is a gap of eleven years before there is any further mention of 'extra land' and it has to be assumed that something went wrong (the War wasn't far off) and the offer was not taken up. At a meeting on 25th October 1923 John Keiller Greig and Major Milne were appointed to see the Factor regarding the renewal of the lease and additional ground but it wasn't until the AGM in April 1924 that the members learned of the conditions for the new lease from Major Milne:

(1)That Mr Farquharson takes possession of all property . . . according to the terms of the lease now expiring.

(2)That the new lease be for a term of 14 years at an annual rent of £55 plus £15 for the extra land [27 acres].

(3)The proprietor to relieve the Club of Owner's Taxes.

(4)That in addition to the arable land pointed out to the Committee, he is prepared to recommend that the Club get as much of the rough ground in front of Beauvais as it may require for the purpose of making more sporting greens and tees.

(5)All grass and crop to be taken over by the Club at valuation from Mr [Peter] Mitchell same as an ordinary agricultural tenant.

The Members voted to accept the new lease and the Club now turned its attention to finding an architect to design the new layout. They decided to write to Mr T. Simpson, of Bramshot, Hampshire, Dr A. McKenzie of Moor Allerton Lodge, Leeds and Mr James Braid, now at Walton Heath. Following receipt of quotations the Club decided to appoint Dr McKenzie and it was agreed that if he approved an additional nine-hole course would be added.

Under Dr McKenzie's direction the British Golf Course Construction Co. (BGCCC) commenced work. In December 1924 as a safeguard against the Club being unable to meet all the costs it was arranged that five members would guarantee £50 each. They were Lt. Col John Milne, the Provost, J. Keiller Greig, Mr J. Lumsden, Mr C. Stewart, and Mr W.W. Tytler.

In June 1925 a meeting of the Committee decided unanimously that the BGCCC work should be discontinued. No reason is given for this action but it is clear from later minutes that although the design work had been completed the construction of the new holes was not finished.

Work continues through 1925 and 1926, presumably under local supervision, and at the AGM in 1927:

> Mr Lumsden proposed a vote of thanks to the Captain, John Keiller Greig, for his gift of a plan of the new course. Two scoring cards, one with map and rules, were submitted to the meeting and approved. [There was to be a charge of one penny for the card with the plan and a half-penny for the other.]

The meeting agreed that the present Green fees included permission to play on the nine-hole course and it was announced that the new course would be opened on Thursday 26th May.

*　　　　　*　　　　　*

At this point Sluievannachie farm has all but disappeared. 'Sluie' Mitchell had died in 1922 and it was his son Peter who enabled the Club to take over almost all the remaining land so that the course could be extended to 27 holes. Old Sluie's tenancy also included the field which lies on the left at the west end of the Pass of Ballater where it meets the Braemar Road. This used to be known as Mrs Shepherd's park—it was there she walked her dogs. Mrs Shepherd lived in a wooden house which, having been burnt down, was replaced by the present Craigendarroch Hotel built by Jo Keiller in 1891.

*　　　　　*　　　　　*

Shortly after the War started in 1939 most of the ground occupied by the nine-hole course was requisitioned and used for stabling horses. A saw-mill was also brought into use. After the War the land was sold to the Council, a Fire Station was built on it and the remainder became the Caravan Park of today. The Golf Club struggled through the fifties gaining strength from increased membership, growing prosperity, and the increased popularity of the game. By the time George Smith became Captain in 1964 the Club was ready to move forward—plans for improvements to the Clubhouse and the course began to take shape.

The work of altering the course was carried out by the greenkeeping staff to a design which had been worked out by the Club Council under George's Captaincy. However the precaution was taken to have the new layout inspected by a Golf Course Architect and the fee paid (£75) was virtually a reward for approving the scheme put forward by the Club! The 1967 Club Championship was the last to be played over the old course; thereafter the new holes were gradually brought into play.

Twenty years later, in 1986, the sequence of holes was altered

26

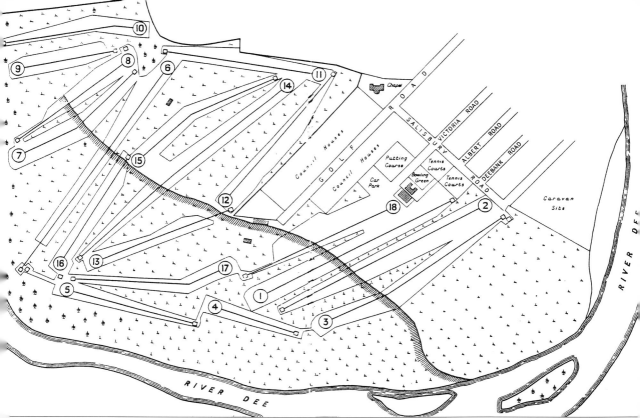

The eighteen hole course from 1927 to 1967. Until World War II there was a nine hole course within the caravan park and the land just south west of it.

between the 6th and the 15th, and this has proved popular since it gives the player who has all but ruined his card in the tough opening stretch, an opportunity to rescue the situation and enter the Clubhouse, if not totally triumphant, at least not filled with the customery despair.

THE PURCHASE OF THE COURSE

At the half year meeting on 26th October 1964 Norman McLeod proposed that the Club start negotiations with a view to purchasing the course. This was carried by a majority and later it was agreed that Alan Watt of Gray and Kellas should be approached.

The Council met on 11th February 1965:

Purchase of course. The Chairman read out letters received from Mr Alan Watt. . . . Captain Farquharson was not prepared to sell until the Club's lease expired. The Club could, however, submit what they considered a keen offer and this would receive consideration. In the meantime the Burgh of Ballater were negotiating for the purchase of the Caravan site,

27

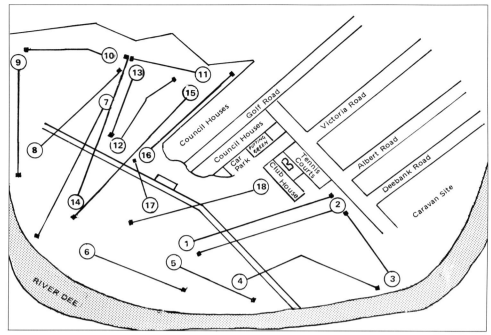

The 1967 changes brought some of the unused land to the south west of the caravan park into use and lengthened the course from 5814 yards to 6094 yards.

and it was decided to try and find out what this price was.

The matter was raised again at a Club meeting in October when the Chairman reported that the Invercauld estate were still unwilling to commit themselves to a price and in any case the Club might have difficulty in raising a loan. He proposed that a deputation should meet Captain Farquharson in the Spring.

At the A.G.M. held in April 1966 the latest position was out-lined as follows:

> The Estate was not interested in a sale at present and suggested a new lease for twenty years commencing Whitsunday 1966. The new lease would have a break at ten years. The rent at commencement would be £300 with five year reviews.

The members didn't particularly like the proposals and agreed that negotiations should continue.

By October the situation had hardened a little, the Chairman of the Club meeting announced that Invercauld was now proposing a rental of £350!

However by the end of November matters had improved. Mr Hay,

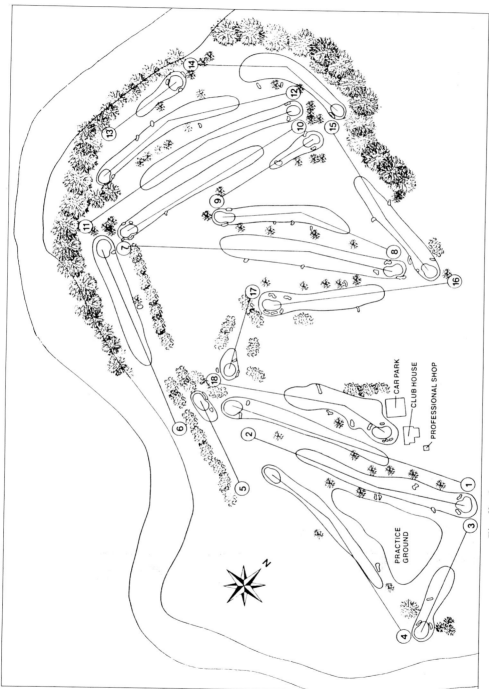

Finally the sequence of holes was altered in 1987 to the present layout.

Treasurer, read out a letter he had received from Alan Watt who had had a discussion with the Invercauld Legal Agents at which he had suggested, as a basis for negotiation, a purchase price of £10,000 to £12,000. The Club was now advised to await Captain Farquharson's reaction.

Alan Watt attending a Council meeting on 17th April 1967 said that the price given by Captain Farquharson was £12,500 and that he had made an application for a Grant [the Scottish Education Department dealt with these matters in those days] although the maximum Grant obtainable was £10,000. He thought the Ballater Town Council could be approached for an additional Grant.

The Council held a meeting on 6th May 1968 to review the latest situation. The Education Department had written to the effect that it was prepared to make a grant not exceeding £9,850. The estimated cost of purchasing the course and altering the Clubhouse was put at £24,150.

One of the conditions of sale imposed by Invercauld, was the retention of the fishing rights and one yard of the river bank. This brought up the question of erosion and Mr Watt undertook to get the position regarding this yard properly defined.

In June it was reported that the Town Council agreed to grant a loan repayable over a period of ten or twelve years at a rate of interest the same as the Council had to pay to the Public Works Loan Board—at present a shade under 8%.

In July Mr Watt was asked to go ahead with the purchase of the course and suggesting that a clause be included protecting the Club on the matter of the erosion of the bank.

In October at a Club meeting the Captain (Harry Wright) announced that the course would be purchased on 28th November for £12,000. (The reduction from £12,500 was a measure of generosity on the part of the Laird who met Harry by chance in Braemar one day. Harry made the point that a reduction in the price would be a great help to the Club which was very short of cash.) The Captain went on to say that the Education Department would then pay the Club £6,000. No explanation is given for the reduction in the grant.

At the A.G.M. in March 1969 the Captain was able to report that the Club had had a very successful year. The course had been purchased from Invercauld and work on erosion at the river bank appeared to have been a success.

And so the matter disappears from the minutes.

THREE

The Pavilion

In 1905 faced with the costs of extending the course, taking on additional staff, and constructing a new Clubhouse the committees and members spent much time on fund raising activities. Letters were sent to a number of people inviting them to become Patrons (Appendix One) and there is evidence that some subscribed to the Club. But it became necessary to remind others and at a meeting in June 1905 it was agreed to adopt more energetic methods:

> it was decided to hold a house to house collection. The Secretary was instructed to write to the Aboyne and Banchory Golf Clubs asking for a copy of notices sent round prior to making such a collection . . . a donation of £10 should confer Life Membership.

During the Summer of 1905 a meeting of the Committee of Management decided to close the new part of the course on Friday 25th August since the Highland Games were being held on it. The committee also deputed Mr Alex Knox, of MacQueen & Knox, Advocates, Aberdeen, to see Mr M.M. Duncan of the Royal Aberdeen Golf Club, to discuss the question of an expert being brought in to advise the Club as to the plan of the new course, size of greens and the position of a new Pavilion.

M.M. Duncan was a scratch golfer at his best. He was Secretary of the Royal Aberdeen Golf Club from 1893 to 1921 and then Captain in 1921.

On 27th September Mr Knox wrote that Mr Duncan and Archie Simpson proposed to visit the course next day:

> Mr Duncan is to motor out and Mr Simpson will arrive [by train] at 11.48 . . . it was agreed that all available committee members should meet the two to conduct them over the ground and give them all necessary information.

Messrs Duncan and Simpson were also assisting in the selection of a permanent full-time Greenkeeper. For his services to the Club Archie Simpson was voted an honorarium of £2–2–0.

In November William Proctor proposed that the Club should proceed with the new Clubhouse having in view its use as a pavilion by bowlers and tennis players. Regarding the siting of the Clubhouse Mr Jebb was asked to call upon Mr Farquharson of Invercauld when in London for the purpose of discussing the matter with him.

During March 1906 plans and specifications for a pavilion 52′×30′ with a verandah all round were submitted by W. Duguid & Son, Grant Bros., and Gordon, of Drochet. The Club accepted Mr James Grant's plan. Mr Proctor offered to ask George Logie, Andrew Carnegie's architect for the rebuilt and enlarged Skibo Castle, (formerly Schytherbolle Castle), west of Dornoch, to give specifications for building at minimum cost.

At meetings of the Committee of Management:

It was agreed that the Secretary instruct the Treasurer to write lax subscribers stating in the most courteous manner possible that the Committee would be greatly favoured by payment of their promised contributions.

It was intimated that Mr Smith, the Factor, had offered the Club an 18 year lease on a plot of ground 160′×400′ between Albert Road and Victoria Road to the west of Salisbury Road for the Pavilion—the Club accepted. It was decided [contrary to the prior decision] to proceed with the Pavilion without reference to bowling or tennis.

... agreed that the Golf Club proceed at once to borrow £300 for the erection of a golf Pavilion ... and that the Club authorize their committee to ask as many members as possible to go security for said sum; while the property of the Club viz: Revenue, Houses, Greens etc. shall stand as security to the Guarantors—who shall number not less than twelve—of the £300 until it is redeemed.

On 5th April the Secretary wrote to the Banks in Ballater:

I am instructed ... to inform you that we purpose borrowing about £300 for the erection of a Club House, upon the personal security of at least twelve prominent members of the Club to be afterwards named.

It is proposed to hold a Bazaar in 1907 in order to clear off the debt. It is to be understood that the Club may reduce the loan from time to time by instalments. The Committee are taking in quotations for rate of interest ... and they will be glad to hear from you stating your lowest terms.

During April George Logie had written from Inverness enclosing a plan for the Clubhouse and it was agreed that Mr Proctor would wire him that it was satisfactory and asking him to proceed with the specifications. It was agreed that a £300 loan at 5% from the Union Bank would be the best policy.

33

LEFT *The pavilion designed and built in 1906.*

Arrangements concerning the new Pavilion, the Bazaar, and the formal opening of the course were to be left to the appropriate committees.

The Committee met on 11th May 1906 and Tenders for the Pavilion were opened. Mr J.D. Brebner of Aboyne had submitted £487 and this was accepted but it was resolved to retain 5% of the price for one year as a guarantee of the upkeep of the building. (In October 1913 it was agreed to install electric lighting.)

Several meetings are held before August 16:

The Great North of Scotland Railway donates £10 as promised.

A letter from Major Malcolm Murray, Equerry to H.R.H. the Duke of Connaught is read intimating that H.R.H. the Duchess of Connaught had graciously consented to honour the proposed Bazaar of 1907 with her Patronage.

It is agreed to have the Pavilion insured for £500, furniture and fittings £100, and member's property £150.

Discussion took place with regard to a proposal that members should pay 6d annually for insurance on material in their lockers . . . no decision.

Mr H.G.Anderson, the President, makes it known that he wishes to entertain about 70 gentlemen to Lunch in the Invercauld Arms on the day of the opening of the Pavilion and extended course.

*   *   *

Many years later, at the half-year meeting of the Club on 21st September 1960, it was reported:

The Council, having considered the inadequate accommodation now provided in the Clubhouse, had obtained a plan of reconstruction drawn up by Mr Irvine, architect, Banchory, and this was passed round. The main alteration was an extension of the building out to the verandah pillars right round the clubhouse to give about double the floor space in the main club room and an opportunity of providing larger locker rooms and toilets and the addition of a kitchen and storeroom . . . the whole work would cost about £2000.

Provost Anderson put forward a different solution but, after discussion, it was agreed to accept the architect's plan and to appoint a sub-committee to go into the whole matter.

The Secretary said he expected to have about £1000 in hand at the end of the winter, and if the Club gave him permission to sell the £300 3% War Stock he thought the balance could be borrowed from the Bank. He added that he thought the overdraft could be cleared by August 1961.

An E.G.M. was held on 22nd November 1961. The cost of the alterations had now risen to £2700 but it was agreed to proceed immediately. The Bank loan would now be £2000.

Ian Paterson, the Club Captain, with Andy Stewart who performed the ceremony on the occasion of the opening of the clubhouse extension in March 1978.

The proposed loan was to be guaranteed by ten members each for £200 to be repaid over a period of three years.

During 1962 the work of altering the Clubhouse must have proceeded at a gentle pace because it is not until February 1963 that the final accounts are presented for payment.

In August 1963 the Council decides to consider the purchase of Craigard (House) Hotel which was on the market.

In November 1966 there is the mention of further alterations 'to be carried out in two phases at an approximate cost of £8,000'. Later in the sixties there is the first mention of the possibility of building one or two houses on the old tennis courts. Planning permission was obtained but in the event the members decided to spend the money on clubhouse improvement.

*   *   *

There are no further clubhouse developements until July 1974 when the most ambitious improvement scheme of all gets under way. An architect from Aberdeen is invited to attend a meeting and various suggestions are put to him. He agrees to draw up outline plans including plans for two semi-detached houses on the old tennis courts (again!).

35

In August some provisional figures are provided by the architect. Modernising the property and adding an additional floor would cost £60,000 to £80,000. Building one house would cost £10,000, two houses £18,000. Following considerable discussion it was agreed that two houses should be built on the old tennis courts.

At the AGM in March 1975, however, it was announced that the Aberdeen County Council had turned down planning permission for the houses but there was to be an appeal. The view of the meeting was that, given permission, the Club should proceed with the houses but holding any action on the Clubhouse until plans for the bar alterations were submitted—hopefully in time for the six monthly meeting to be held later in the year.

At the half-yearly meeting in September it is announced that Planning permission has been granted for the two houses. (At the same meeting it is agreed that Annual Subscriptions for men should be raised to £9!).

'Two-houses' appears in the minutes frequently through 1975 as estimates are adjusted but the indications are that the project is doomed. Ian Paterson, upon his election as Captain in 1976, says that his project for the next three years would be the improvement of the clubhouse and with this in mind he proposed having a major raffle to raise funds. And a new possibility rears its head. Balgonie, a large house near the 14th green has come on the market at a price of £45,000 and it has a self-contained flat, eliminating the necessity to build the houses. A sub-committee is formed and a Special Meeting called for 31st May.

At the meeting it is clear that (a) Balgonie was unsuitable and (b) the Council now took the view that the houses should not be built. Permission was, however, granted to employ an architect to draw up a five-stage plan for the developement of the clubhouse.

In September 1975 it is now reckoned that the costs had risen to over £100,000. The Council applied for Grants from The Sports Council and the Scottish Tourist Board but without success!

The Clubhouse extension gradually got under way and it must have been a very frustrating time for some members of the Club Council. Ian Paterson remembers that during one twelve month period he attended no less that 82 meetings at which the building work was discussed.

In the event the Club decided to restrict the extension to phase one only, spending about £72,000, and leaving phase two to the future. Phase one included the new member's lounge and bar upstairs and it had been intended to erect a similar extension at the other end of the building. This would have provided accommodation for Club staff.

The official opening ceremony was carried out by Andy Stewart on 3rd March 1978.

36

FOUR

Braid vs Vardon

The Committee met on 11th May 1906. Regarding the formal opening of the course it was agreed that Mr J.H. Anderson (Greenkeeper) would ask James Braid to procure the services of another noted professional, Harry Vardon if possible, and arrange a date for the match. Terms were to be £10 and expenses.

By the middle of July arrangements had been made for the match (Braid vs Vardon) to take place on 16th August and steps were taken to advertise the event in the Press. Rooms for Braid and Vardon were booked at the Invercauld Arms Hotel. The Club undertook to give the Railway Company the necessary guarantee for 200 adult passengers or equivalent. Admission to the course on the day was to be 1/- and a notice was to be displayed requesting members and visitors to leave the course free until the evening.

Four additional constables are engaged at 5/- each and expenses.

Mrs Anderson of Oakhall accepts the invitation to open the course by driving a ball from the first tee. The Council decides to present Mrs Anderson with a golf club with silver plate thereon suitably inscribed for the purpose of driving the first ball.

Thus the stage was set for the great match.

*   *   *

On the morning of Thursday 16th August 1906 *The Aberdeen Free Press* carried the following items on the Sports page:

GOLF IN RUSSIA

The first Golf Club in Russia has opened on the Kolomiaghi racecourse just outside St Petersburg. The course stretching for 2640 yards, has nine holes, the longest of which is 500 yards. Count Nirod is President and the Honorary members include the British and Italian Ambassadors and the Swedish Minister.

The opening match was a foursome between Princess Volkousky and Mr Percy Henderson (British Embassy) and Mrs H.S. King and Mr M.A. Zoppi, the Hon. Secretary. The former [pair] won, the Princess starting off with a fine drive.

BRAID AND VARDON AT BALLATER

Braid and Vardon arrived at Ballater yesterday afternoon.... In the evening they played a preliminary round in view of todays match. The players were in splendid form and gave a capital display. Vardon led by one hole at the ninth with a score of 37, Braid being 39. Vardon continued to play the better game and kept the upper hand, and at the end won by three holes, his score being 68 against 71. The bogey for the course is 75.

*   *   *

In the Summer of 1906 James Braid and Harry Vardon were arguably the two best golfers in the world.

Braid was born in Elie, Fife, on 6th February 1870. He died on 27th November 1950 at the age of 80. He was an honorary member of the Royal and Ancient and of Walton Heath golf club where he was professional for 45 years. A joiner by trade, Braid played as an amateur in Fife and Edinburgh. In 1893 he went to London and worked as a club-maker. A tall powerful player, 'he lashed the ball with *divine* fury!' (*Golfer's Handbook*).

Vardon was born in Grouville, Jersey, 9th May 1870. He was the professional at Ganton for seven years until he became ill in 1903. He then became professional at the South Herts Club in Totteridge where he remained until his death on 20th March 1937. Vardon was the inventor of the orthodox 'Vardon grip'. He was Open champion six times.

At the time of their appearance at Ballater Vardon had already won the Open four times and the U.S. Open once. Braid had won the Open three times including his recent win at Muirfield in June where Vardon was third behind Braid and J.H. Taylor.

*   *   *

The encounter at Ballater had been preceded by a 36 hole match at Dornoch on 14th August. *Golf Illustrated*:

Neither player had seen the course before ... Dornoch was *en fete* for the occasion, and as the enterprising Highland Railway ran special trains ... and the weather was beautiful ... the match was followed by a gallery of over 1000 people.

N John Beaton Esq

6th July 1906

Memorandum from **JAMES BRAID,**

OPEN CHAMPION, 1901.
" " 1905.
" " 1906.

WALTON HEATH GOLF CLUB,
WALTON-ON-THE-HILL.
STATION :—
Tadworth, S.E.Ry.
Surrey.

Telegrams :—"BRAID, GOLF, WALTON-ON-THE-HILL."

PARCELS :—Tadworth Station, S.E.Ry.

GOLF CLUB and
BALL MAKER.

Speciality: DRIVERS and BRASSIES.

Dear Sir,
In reply to yours of the 3rd I beg to say the terms offered by your club are quite acceptable with £10 each and expenses. Thanking you very much for invitation

Yours Respectfully
Jas Braid

Letters from James Braid and Harry Vardon.

Telegrams—"Vardon, Golf Club, Totteridge."
Station—Totteridge, G.N.R.

Memo from ..

H. VARDON,

Golf Club & Ball Maker.

Golf Clubs of Persimmon, Dogwood and Beech.

ALL ORDERS GIVEN BEST ATTENTION.   MONTHLY ACCOUNTS.

South Herts Golf Club,
Totteridge,
London, N.,
190 6

To ....

Open Champion 1896-98-99.
1903. American Champion
1900, and winner of 41 First
Class Tournaments.

The only Golfer who has
ever won both English
and American Champion-
ships.

Dear Sir,
Letter to hand with thanks we will arrive the day before the match no doubt have a practice round.

Yours truly
Harry Vardon

THE ABERDEEN FREE PRESS, FRIDAY, AUGUST 17, 1906

BRAID—VARDON MATCH AT BALLATER

*

Opening of extended course

*

Brilliant play by Braid

*

The extended course of the Ballater Golf Club was formally opened for play yesterday, when the interesting occasion was marked by an exhibition match of 36 holes between James Braid, the Open champion, and Harry Vardon, the ex-champion. . . .

The formal opening of the handsome new Clubhouse was the first ceremonial function. This took place at eleven o'clock, in the presence of a very large gathering of ladies and gentlemen, there being a large representation of the visitors to the district as well as a considerable number of people from Aberdeen and Deeside.

In making their preparations for the opening of the course the committee . . . had arranged with the Great North of Scotland Railway Company to run a special train from Aberdeen . . . its arrival at Ballater brought between 200 and 300 people anxious to witness the match between the champion and his formidable rival. The artistic clubhouse was beautifully decorated. . . . Right round the structure was a pretty display of flags and bannerettes, while over the entrance was a profusion of pine foliage and stags' heads, the latter having been kindly lent for the occasion by Mr John Findlay, taxidermist. It had been originally arranged that the clubhouse should be formally opened by Sir Allan MacKenzie of Glenmuick. Unfortunately he was ill and was unable to fulfil the engagement, his place being kindly taken by Mr Victor MacKenzie, his eldest surviving son . . . accompanied by his brother-in-law, Lord Kilmarnock. [Sir Allan MacKenzie died on 20th August. His son Victor, born in 1882, a Lieut. in the 3rd Bn. Scots Guards, succeeded him. Lord Kilmarnock had married Mary Lucy Victoria, daughter of Sir Allan MacKenzie.]

Opening the proceedings Mr H.G. Anderson, Oakhall, President of the Club, referred to the unfortunate circumstance which prevented Sir Allan MacKenzie being present. He said he was sure they all joined in the hope that Sir Allan would soon be restored to good health—(applause). It was exceedingly gratifying, however, that Sir Allan's son, Mr Victor MacKenzie, had kindly taken his father's place that day, and he had pleasure . . . in calling upon him to open their pavilion.

Mr MacKenzie, thanked the Club for the honour they had done him in asking him to take the place of his father . . . He should rather thank them for asking Lord Kilmarnock or himself to open the clubhouse. They were both anxious to come, and as they could not settle it otherwise they drew lots and the honour fell upon himself. (Laughter and applause.)

He referred in complimentary terms to the excellent clubhouse which had been provided, as showing the excellence of the arrangements that had been made by the committee, and said that golf, as everyone knew, was now a very important and popular national game, while Ballater was also one of the most popular health resorts in the country—(app). Not only would that clubhouse be appreciated by the inhabitants of Ballater, but it would be recognised as a great convenience by the visitors. Ballater was always to the fore in everything—(app). It was only natural that having made such an excellent course they should also have a first rate clubhouse. Ballater people did not do things by halves—(app). They were just about to witness a match between Braid and Vardon, whose skill they had all heard about. That was therefore a most fitting and memorable occasion and one that would always be remembered—(app). He could only say that he hoped the Ballater Club would get their reward for their enterprise and trouble, and that the . . . course would become more largely patronised than ever. . . . He had great pleasure in declaring the clubhouse open—(app).

Mr H.G. Anderson said that as President of that Club, he had been asked by the committee to open that beautiful course, and they had also been good enough to ask Mrs Anderson to hit off the first ball. He could assure them that they both felt it a great honour. . . .

Mr Anderson afterwards paid a tribute to the arduous labours of the members of the committee and others, including the Captain of the Club, Mr H.S.F. Jebb in connection with the undertaking the successful realisation of which they had seen that day. They were also much indebted to Mr Farquharson of Invercauld and his factor, Mr Smith. . . . As Mr MacKenzie had said, Ballater would always be to the front. From time immemorial it had been a health resort, and it was now asserting its position as a pleasure resort—(app). In these progressive days it could not afford to stand still, and he trusted that the extended course was only one step towards further recreative facilities such as a tennis court and a bowling green—(app). Referring to the match . . . Mr Anderson said the names of Braid and Vardon were household words, and they were true sportsmen . . . they not only went to the grand places, but came to such courses as theirs to help the weakling, and they were exceedingly indebted to them. . . . The world would now know that Ballater had a proper golf course and he was sure it would redound to the benefit of the Town. He had pleasure in declaring the golf course open.

Provost Barnett said he had been asked to perform the very pleasant duty of introducing to them Mrs Anderson of Oakhall. She was well known to the people of Ballater, and he was sure, after that day's proceedings, all would wish to know her and none would forget her—(app). The Club had been very fortunate in their president and all their officials, and they were doubly so in having Mrs Anderson there to drive off the first ball—(app). Before that he had to ask her to accept, from the members, a beautiful club, which bore the inscription: 'Presented to Mrs H.G. Anderson of Oakhall on the formal opening of the extended golf course. Ballater, 16th August, 1906'. He hoped that Mrs Anderson would be able, by the aid of that club, to give the President many a good beating—(great laughter and app).

Mr Anderson thanked the club on behalf of Mrs Anderson. The club, which was a beautiful piece of workmanship, was made by Mr Forgan of St Andrews, and supplied by Mr Willox, of Ballater.

Mr H.S.F. Jebb, Captain, proposed a vote of thanks to Mr Victor MacKenzie for opening the clubhouse, to Mr Anderson for presiding, and to Mrs Anderson for the duty she was to perform in driving off the first ball.

Mr Victor Mackenzie acknowledged . . . this part of the proceedings closed, and the company adjourned to the course. . . . At the close of the first round . . . Braid and Vardon . . . and a large company of guests were entertained at a sumptuous luncheon in Mr Proctor's Invercauld Arms Hotel, by the President of the Club, Mr H.G. Anderson and the Vice-President, Mr Yarrow. Mr Anderson presided, and Mr H.S.F. Jebb, Captain of the Club, was croupier.

Mr J.B. Rennett proposed 'Prosperity to the Ballater Golf Club'. He said that whatever else might be thought of the . . . course it was certainly the most beautifully situated in the kingdom. He also remarked that in

London Offices : 173, 174, 175 FLEET STREET, LONDON, E.C.	Telegraphic Addresses :	Press Telegrams : GOLF REPORTING AGENCY, LONDON. Inland Telegrams : - "JASPILITE," LONDON.	Telephone : 1698 HOLBORN, LONDON.

The Golf Reporting Agency,
8 North Bridge,
Edinburgh, August. 4th. 190 6.

Telegraphic Addresses :
Inland Telegrams :
"RAPID," EDINBURGH.
Press Telegrams :
PRESS AGENCY, EDINBURGH.
Telephone :
1380 EDINBURGH.

THE GOLF REPORTING AGENCY has Correspondents at every Golf Links at Home and Abroad, and is the only Agency devoted entirely to Reporting Golf.
Official Publishers of " The Golfer's Handbook and Year Book " and " The Ladies' Golf Union Year Book."

Dear Sir,

With regard to the Braid-Vardon match to be held at your links, we wish to make special arrangements regarding the reporting of the same. We would want a sixpenny wire sent off at the third, ninth, and eighteenth holes in both rounds. Could you arrange with some local party to do this for us? Of course, we would want same despatched promptly. We will be glad to receive your reply by return when we will send you particular details of what we require.

Yours faithfully,

The Golf Reporting Agency.

John Beaton. Esq.

Ballater Golf Club.

Ballater.

carrying out the improvements a great deal of expense had been incurred, and it was the intention to hold a bazaar next year to aid in wiping off the debt.... Amid loud applause, he said that a member of the Royal Family had graciously consented to give her patronage to the Bazaar. He coupled the toast with the name of the Captain of the Club, Mr Jebb—(app).

Mr Jebb responding in an eloquent speech, said that they could offer every justification for the outlay they had incurred, because if Ballater was not absolutely up-to-date in the way of being able to offer its visitors a good golf course and a good pavilion, etc., it was quite possible that it would be beaten by its neighbouring rivals at Braemar and Aboyne.

Rev. Father Mathieson proposed the health of the President of the Club, and Mr Anderson acknowledged.

The course in 1906 as described in the Bazaar (1907) booklet:

Out	Yards	Bogey	In	Yards	Bogey
1 The Coyles	358	5	10 Balmoral	312	4
2 Salisbury	303	4	11 Birkhall	252	4
3 Garranmohr	268	4	12 Sluievannachie	255	4
4 Spinning Jenny	314	4	13 Old Clubhouse	241	5
5 Manse	214	4	14 The Neuk	199	3
6 Saddle Back	300	5	15 Dark Lochnagar	283	4
7 Long Hole	372	5	16 Brackley	205	4
8 Island	104	3	17 Lochnagar White	188	4
9 Glenmuick	291	5	18 Home Hole	233	4
Total out	2524	39	Total in	2168	36

Length 4692 yards. Bogey 75.

The first tee is to the south-east of the Clubhouse, and the hole is directly westwards. It is appropriately called The Coyles, for as one progresses thither a glorious vista is opened up with the Coyles o' Muick in the distance, directly in the line of view from the tee to the putting green. It is plain sailing to within 50 yards of the green, which is immediately approached by roughish and undulating ground, which adds a spice of variety to the situation, and requires neat pitching to negotiate.

For the second hole the player turns directly eastward. It is over the new ground and is called the Salisbury, because it lies directly short of Salisbury Terrace.

The third hole rejoices in the distinctly picturesque name of Garran-mohr, derived from an historic house in Ballater situated in the neighbourhood. It is still further eastward over the new ground, and the view ahead is superb, the stately wooded height of Craig-Coilach to the south-east filling the eye all the time.

The player then turns westward. He has to tackle the hole called Spinning Jenny, a name suggested by the fact that play lies along the course of the Spinning Jenny burn.

Pushing still westward, with the Parish Church Manse (now Invermuick) facing one, just beyond the junction of the Dee and the Muick we have the Manse hole.

43

The sixth is the Saddle Back, and lies back in the middle of the new ground.

Now we come to the longest hole in the course—the Long Hole. It is played directly westward from the Saddle Back, bringing the eyes of the player back to the gorgeous mountain scenery; he has the pleasant prospect of getting back, with two good shots, on to natural turf again.

The eighth is the shortest hole. It is called the Island, because the putting green is actually on an island beyond a water course, frequently quite dry, but none the less an absolute trap for the nervous player. The hole is only 104 yards in length—just a pitch from the tee.

The ninth hole, Glenmuick, lies directly northward from the Island, along the western side of the old course with its excellent natural turf. The name Glenmuick comes naturally to one on this green, for, turning our eyes to the south-west, we can see the stately mansion house of the MacKenzie's, in the distant, glorious woodland.

The tenth hole is the Balmoral, for now we direct our steps to a point which is perhaps nearest to, though still far away, from the Royal Highland home. It runs northwards from the Glenmuick hole.

The eleventh also claims an historic name. It is the Birkhall hole, and lies directly south from the Balmoral hole.

For the twelfth hole we turn back, northwards. It is called Sluievanna-chie, and lifting our eyes as we go, we see the valley of the Gairn sweeping away towards the watershed between Don and Dee, with nearer and more definite scenic touches filling up a striking panorama of natural beauty.

The thirteenth is called the Old Clubhouse, as the putting green lies southwards, opposite the little shanty which in the old days served as a clubhouse for the golfers of Ballater. Today, it is a handy shelter for the unfortunate player who may be caught in a thunder-shower in the vicinity.

The fourteenth hole is well named the Neuk. It lies on the new ground, almost directly eastward from the last green.

Playing to the fifteenth green we turn westward, the ultimate goal of our ambition for the moment being again well into the old natural course. This hole is called Dark Lochnagar, suggested no doubt by the westward view, for the 'dark, frowning' summit of historic Lochnagar may be seen peeping up behind the nearer Coyles.

From the fifteenth green one plays southward—still keeping to the natural ground—towards Brackley House, which may be seen nestling in the woodland beyond the Dee.

From Brackley one turns towards the north, and plays for the fifteenth green again which, being a double one, serves also for the seventeenth.

The Home hole lies short of the Clubhouse, directly eastward from the 17th.

It is characteristic of the enterprise of the Club that last holiday season was no sooner at an end than they proceeded to improve the course. The putting-greens were carefully nursed and tended through the winter months, five new ones were laid, and the judicious distribution of artificial bunkers on the new ground has added a spice of sport to the course which it did not possess before.

44

THE MATCH

The first round of the match of 36 holes between Braid and Vardon was to have started at half-past eleven o'clock, but it was delayed considerably beyond that hour owing to a breakdown in the weather. The sky had been overcast in the morning, and while the ceremony of opening the new clubhouse was in progress there were frequent peals of thunder and a heavy downpour of rain. By noon the rainfall lightened considerably, and a start was made with the match.

By this time a very large crowd of people had arrived from Aberdeen and the more populous centres on Deeside.... Just before the professionals drove off there was an interesting little ceremony, Mrs Anderson, with the beautiful club presented to her in the pavilion, driving off the first ball. This she did most gracefully and her well-hit shot at once disclosed a prior acquaintance with the game ... [it] was greeted with a hearty cheer.

Vardon took the honour at the first tee, and at the green the champion (Braid), with a mashie pitch from outside the turf, holed out in 3—two under par—and won the hole amid applause. He increased his lead to two holes at the second, where a pitched third by Vardon broke on the edge of the green, and the latter required 5 to Braid's 4. Four halves in 4 followed. Going to the seventh, which is the longest hole in the course—407 yards—Vardon was in the whins to the left with his second, and required two to get on the green. Braid ran his third to the lip of the hole, won in 4 and stood three up. The eighth hole is the shortest in the course, being only a hundred yards, but it is exceedingly tricky, demanding very accurate play. It was halved in 4.

After good drives to the ninth, Braid, with a beautiful pitch from beside a small pool of water, placed his ball within a foot or two of the hole, and won by getting down in three. Vardon ... took 4.

Braid thus turned 4 holes up on the match, his score for the nine holes being 34 to Vardon's approximate 39.

Vardon won his first hole at the eleventh where he got down in 3 to Braid's 4. At the twelfth, however the champion again became four up, Vardon pitching his second over the green, while Braid was down in three. The thirteenth was halved in four while the Neuk was halved in three. At the fifteenth (Dark Lochnagar) Vardon pushed his second to the right of the green and failed to get down in four, Braid won the hole and stood five up on the match. At the sixteenth Braid's drive lay in casual water and he had to lift and drop. He pitched perfectly and was down in 3. Vardon had no difficulties but he left himself too long a putt and he lost the hole. Braid was now six up. After a half in 3 at the seventeenth, Vardon got down in 3 to Braid's 4 at the eighteenth. The first round thus ended with the open champion in the lead by five holes. The approximate details of the round were:

Braid	out	3–4–4–4–4–4–4–4–3	34	
	in	4–4–3–4–3–4–3–3–4	32	Total 66

| Vardon | out | 4–5–4–4–4–4–6–4–4 | 39 | |
| | in | 4–3–4–4–3–5–4–3–3 | 33 | Total 72 |

Braid's round of 66 was a magnificent performance. He played through-out with great, good judgement and delighted the spectators with his beautiful approach play and putting, the latter being remarkably accurate. Vardon did not seem to be playing with the confidence which he has often shown. His old automatic exactness seemed to be wanting, though his style of play was quite as pretty as ever.

THE SECOND ROUND

Before the start of the second round, the professionals, together with some of the officials of the club and others were photographed in front of the pretty clubhouse. The weather by this time had cleared up considera-bly and the second round was played under more pleasant conditions. Again there was a very large crowd of spectators, and every stroke in the game was followed with the closest possible interest.

At the first hole Vardon was past the green with his second, while Braid was short. Braid played his third strong and Vardon, running up nicely with his third, had a chance of the hole in 4, but he missed his putt and the hole was halved. Vardon, lost the second but won the third and with a half at the fourth remained five down.

At the fifth Braid was on the green with a cleek from the tee and ran down in. Vardon short with his drive and his second, just missed the hole with his third, the champion winning the hole in 2 to 4 and six up again. At the Saddleback both players, with long and perfect approaches, halved the hole in 4. At the Long Hole, Vardon pulled his second, pitched poorly, was strong with his fourth and required six. Braid was on in three, won the hole, and stood seven up. At the Short Hole Braid overdrove the green, and Vardon won the hole. The ninth was halved, and Braid, out in 37, turned one up on the round and 6 up on the match. Vardon's score was 39. At Balmoral they halved in four. At Birkhall, Vardon lost the hole pitching too strong and . . . Braid down in 3, won the hole, and stood dormie seven.

At the twelfth Braid was over the green with his second, and Vardon won the hole in 3 to 4 and stood 6 down. The thirteenth was halved in 4, Vardon missing a 3 by the half turn of the ball. The match was now at an end, Braid being the winner by 6 up with 5 to play. The round was played out, and at the fourteenth, Vardon again missing a long putt, lost the hole in 4 to a perfect 3 by the champion. Vardon, however, won the next three holes, in perfect 3's. He lost the last hole in 4 to 3, but he won the bye by a hole. Braid's score for the second round was 70, and Vardon's 71, the details being:

Braid	out	5–4–5–4–2–4–5–4–4	37	
	in	4–3–4–4–3–4–4–4–3	33	Total 70
Vardon	out	5–5–4–4–4–4–6–3–4	39	
	in	4–4–3–4–4–3–3–3–4	32	Total 71

LEFT *16th August 1906 James Braid (left) and Harry Vardon.*

Again, Braid's play was characterised by marvellous accuracy, although he did not succeed in returning the low score he did in the first round. Vardon played a better game than in the first round. He was unfortunate, however, with a number of his putts, his ball often resting on the lip of the hole. His play in the bye was most brilliant, his three 3's in succession for par 4 holes being marvels of accuracy. The arrangements for regulating the crowd during the progress of the match were efficiently attended to by the committee of the club and the local professional, James Anderson, who also deserves credit for the good condition . . . [of the] greens.

On 18th August Harry Vardon played a match at Bieldside with the local professional James Donaldson, while James Braid played a match with Archie Simpson, the Royal Aberdeen professional on the Stonehaven course. At Deeside the scores were, Vardon 67 and 72, Donaldson 66 and 75. At Stonehaven the scores were, Braid 75 and 73, Simpson 75 and 74.

THE PROFESSIONAL

It is important to note that, while extending their course, the Ballater Club also took another step equally necessary to the success of the game at such a popular holiday centre. They appointed a first-class professional, in the person of James Anderson, whose services during the past year in the way of directing and superintending the improvement of the course have been very fully appreciated. Anderson had an excellent upbringing for the position he now occupies. He is the son of Mr David Anderson, the Keeper of the Braids Course, Edinburgh. He worked under his father for a number of years prior to coming to Ballater, and the value of that training will be obvious to all who have seen the magnificently kept course on the Braids. James Anderson is not only thoroughly up in greenkeeping and general management, but is a good club maker and a very neat player. He drives a long, straight ball, pitches accurately, and putts well. With James Anderson as professional, visitors to Ballater, and others, are thus in the enviable position of having not only an expert coach to teach them the game, but one who can provide them with the best class of golfing requisites, and mend their breakages when necessary.

LEFT *16th August 1906 James Braid watches Vardon's putt.*

FIVE

Bazaar and Fancy Fair 16th and 17th August 1907

The Bazaar was held within the Gordon Institute (the building opposite the old Station flanked by the Victoria and Albert Halls). A 48 page booklet was produced for the occasion. It contained 'Golf at Ballater', a plan and description of the Course, a list of the Stalls, and the names of all those who had anything whatsoever to do with the organisation of the day. It also contained a number of advertisements for shops or services most of which no longer exist. Among those that do are the Invercauld Arms (now Monaltrie Hotel), Pannanich Wells Hotel, John Leith & Son, the Bakers, and the Loirston Hotel. The booklet included:

OBJECT OF THE BAZAAR

Considerable debt has been incurred by the improvements which have been carried out on the Course, and its enlargement and extension to eighteen holes, which has been rendered necessary by the growing popularity of the game.

A handsome Pavilion has also been erected for the convenience of the Members and the many Visitors who frequent Ballater during the summer months and take advantage of the Course.

It is the intention of the Committee, if the necessary funds can be raised, to lay out a Bowling Green and Tennis Courts, thereby lending a further attraction to Visitors.

The projected Bazaar, is the only way open to the Club to raise the necessary funds [£800 was the target], and the Committee trusts that members, friends of members, and well-wishers of the Club generally, will respond heartily to this appeal, and so enable the Committee to carry out their proposals.

50

THE BAZAAR COMMITTEE

President: Mr H.G. Anderson, Oakhall, Ballater.

Vice-Presidents: Sir Victor MacKenzie of Glenmuick, Mr R.H.L. Gordon of Abergeldie, Colonel Boyce, Mount Stewart, Ballater, Mr F.J. Yarrow, Newton, Ballater, Mr S. Neumann, Glenmuick.

Captain: Mr H.S.F. Jebb, Tullich Lodge.

Vice-Captains: Rev. D. Matheson, Mr J.D. Littlejohn, Aberdeen, Mr W.J. Thomson.

Secretary: Mr Alick S. Melvin, Ballater.

Treasurer: Mr John Simpson, Ballater.

Committee: Mr D. Birrell, Mr A. Craig, Mr J. Findlay, Mr J. Grant, Mr W.O. Donald, Sergeant Hanna, Mr G.T. Lamond, Mr A. Lowe, Mr W. Proctor, Dr Profeit, Mr J. Smart, Mr Allan Smith, Mr D. Wilkie.

GOLF AT BALLATER

At certain points on the Scottish seaboard the history of the game is represented in centuries, but it is only within comparatively recent years that the tendency of modern recreation has brought the necessity of providing facilities for golf home to the minds of those having an interest in the popularising of our inland health resorts. Keeping this fact in view, we claim for Ballater that it has been thoroughly up-to-date.

For more years than one would venture to guess, those who sought to escape the world's worries in the glorious solitude of mountain, wood, and stream, found Ballater unrivalled, and when old Father Time, with his burden of change, brought golf into the list of recreative necessities, Ballater again was all there. Scenery, of course, is a matter of degree. It is true that the sea can never lack an interest for a healthy mind. Ever changing, it has a fascination all of its own, and along its shores, quite apart from the natural unlimited scope usually available for the proper prosecution of the royal and ancient game, under no other conditions, perhaps, can golf be played with equal invigorating effect. But golf is only one element in the many that go to make up a long and pleasant holiday for all. There is, and ever will be, an unassailable charm for the fagged-out worker in the bracing mountain air associated with the wooded glens of the Scottish Highlands, and particularly fortunate is the holiday centre where one may find a combination of these with now all-important consideration that good natural golfing facilities are available. Ballater is a striking example of such a centre.

But with golf only are we meantime concerned. Over fourteen years ago, the necessity for providing a golf course at Ballater was locally realised and faced. A Golf Club was formed, and steps were at once taken to lay out a course of nine holes. It was a pleasant undertaking, for, unlike many other inland localities designed by nature for the attraction of summer visitors, there was a considerable acreage of natural turf available for the start of the game lying along the north bank of the Dee, conveniently near the Borough, and commanded by scenery unrivalled almost

51

in its natural grandeur. But golf was on the swelling wave of popularity, and it was soon found that a nine hole course was insufficient to meet the demands of the time.

Two years ago, the Club had to face the necessity of obtaining additional ground. By agreement with the superior of the property, Colonel A.H. Farquharson of Invercauld, arrangements were completed whereby the necessary additional ground was acquired between the original course and the Borough of Ballater. No time was lost in having the full course laid out. Very wisely the Club called in the assistance of experts, and Mr M.M. Duncan, Secretary of the Royal Aberdeen Club, and Archie Simpson, the well known professional of the same club gave their advice on the matter. At the same time it was recognised that a suitable clubhouse must be provided. This was done, and now a feature of the neighbourhood is the new clubhouse, a commodious building of artistic design, with pretty verandah facing the course on its eastern side, the red roof of the 'Golfers Rest' contrasting picturesquely with the prevailing green of the surroundings.

Internally, the clubhouse is extremely well arranged. There with spacious windows looking out on the course, is a large clubroom, with a gentlemen's room opening out to the back at one end and a ladies' room at the other.

The extended course was opened in August of last year under the most auspicious circumstances. With characteristic enterprise the Club secured the services of James Braid, the Open Champion, and Harry Vardon for an exhibition match. Such magnificent golf as was witnessed then had never been played before in Aberdeenshire. James Braid went round the course in his opening game with the magnificent score of 66.

An Extraordinary Meeting of the Club and Bazaar Committee was held in the Gordon Institute on 10th September 1907:

H.G. Anderson, the President occupied the Chair. A report was read by Mr Beaton stating that the balance after paying all expenses, loan and interest would amount to about £270 which sum would be available for the formation of a Bowling Green and Tennis Courts. The Chairman moved that the report be adopted. This was seconded by Mr Jebb and agreed.

The Chairman moved that a hearty vote of thanks be given to the Joint Secretaries of the Bazaar Committee. Mr Jebb seconded and the motion was carried unanimously.... Mr Jebb in moving a hearty vote of thanks to the President referred to the great services rendered to the Club by both Mr and Mrs Anderson—much of the success of the Bazaar being due to their united efforts. This was heartily responded to by all present....

A few copies of the Bazaar booklet remain in the village. Mike Sheridan's is one of the most interesting since there are figures on it showing the amounts raised by the Stalls. The writing may be that of John Simpson the Bazaar Treasurer. Stall No. 2 raised £192.8.4 the largest of any. Unfortunately the booklet doesn't reveal what was being sold by

Mrs Anderson, Oakhall, and Mrs Middleton of Heatherbank. H.S.F. Jebb's Book Stall raised £18.11.11 which in those days must have been quite a number of books. According to the back cover the total amount raised was £786.4.11.

BALLATER GOLF CLUB.

GRAND BAZAAR

(In aid of the Funds of the Club),

IN

GORDON INSTITUTE.

On FRIDAY, 16th AUGUST, at Noon,
Mrs. FARQUHARSON, of Invercauld,
will open the Bazaar.

H. G. ANDERSON, ESQ., OAKHALL, WILL PRESIDE.

On SATURDAY, 17th AUGUST, at Noon,
Mrs. COATS, of Glentana, will open the Bazaar.

H. S. F. JEBB, ESQ., TULLICH LODGE, WILL PRESIDE.

Deeside Press, Ballater.

53

ABOVE *James Grant*
BELOW *Henry Scrope Freschville Jebb*

ABOVE *James Will Brockie*
BELOW *John Keiller Greig*

SIX

Presidents, Captains, and Honorary Members

PRESIDENTS

James Grant 1905
H.G. Anderson 1906–1913

At the A.G.M. in May 1913 following the death of H.G. Anderson, John Simpson 'moved that appreciation of the benefits and help rendered to the Club by the late H.G. Anderson be recorded in the Minutes'. The Captain, Dr A.C. Profeit then moved that the offices of President and Vice-President be abolished and the names of Patrons be substituted. The Vice-Presidents of the previous year were then elected Patrons and Mr Alexander Keiller and Mr J.T. Rennie were added.

Henry Gibson Anderson was a Director of the London and River Plate Bank of Buenos Aires. He purchased Oakhall (now the Darroch Learg Annexe) in 1898. In London he lived in Park House, Wimbledon, and was a member of the Oriental Club, Hanover Square. In 1925 Darroch Learg was purchased by Henry Burns Anderson, believed to be H.G. Anderson's son.

CAPTAINS

John Thomas Donald Simpson 1892 to 1902. John Simpson was born in the Parish of Lochlee, Forfarshire. He entered the Union Bank of Scotland in 1863, became Accountant at Ballater in 1874, and succeeded Mr Haynes as Bank Agent in May 1876 with occupancy of the Bank House in Bridge Street. He continued as Agent for the next 42 years until his death on 23rd October 1918 at the age of 72. The Service was held in St Saviour's Church (now St Kentigern's) and he was buried at Tullich. Simpson was Burgh Treasurer and Clerk to the Tullich and Glen Muick School Board. His sister, Margaret Jane, who also lived in the Bank House, died in July 1918. He was Congregational Secretary and Treasurer of St Kentigern's from 1897 until his death and by his will he bequeathed to the Church the sum of £400. John Simpson was the true founder of the Ballater Golf Club.

James Grant 1902 to 1904 and 1913 to 1923. Provost of Ballater 1897 to 1900 and 1915 to 1919. Died 27th March, 1930. Two of his sons farmed the Knocks; both died young, one being killed in action in 1916 at the age of 23. Another son, John, a Half Golf Blue at Aberdeen University, became a doctor and lived most of his life in Orpington, Kent where one of his patients was Bernard Darwin. Two of Grant's grandchildren (daughters of his son George), Sheila (Grant) Farquhar and her sister Lesley Grant became fine golfers. Lesley who is a member of the Scottish Sports Council has her name in any number of slots on the Championship boards at the Banchory Club but there are some who claim that Sheila was the better player. Lesley was denied the opportunity to display her skill on the Ballater course since her application, in 1963, was rejected on the grounds that Banchory was outwith the radius stipulated in Club Rule 25; a rigid application of the rule to a family with such a close association with Ballater.

The youngest son, Joseph who was at one time a member of the Club, was Chaplain with the Black Watch (awarded the M.C. at Monte Cassino) and then appointed to Cromdale Church, Grantown-on-Spey. He died in 1990 at the age of 85. Of Grant's two daughters Grace became the first Captain of the Ladies Section when it was formed in 1930 and Hannah married James Will Brockie, (see below).

James Grant's first wife died in 1916. His second wife Helen Roy died in 1941 at the age 99.

In 1923, when James Grant was succeeded by J. Keiller Greig as Captain, he was elected a Life Member.

William Willox 1904 to 1906. Willox was a cycle agent with premises in Bridge Street and Braemar Road. From an invoice dated July 28, 1906 it is apparent that he also sold golf balls, bags, and clubs. In October 1913 he gave a prize of five clubs to be played for by the members during the winter months. The winner to have the choice of two clubs, the second, the third, and the fourth, to have the choice of one club each.

Henry Scrope Freschville Jebb 1906 to 1910. Henry Jebb lived in Tulloch Lodge, known locally, of course, as Jebb's 'hoose'. He was born on 17th July 1867 at Wickersley, South Yorkshire the son of Rev. Henry Gladwin Jebb and Emma Louisa (daughter of Robert Ramsden of Carlton Hall, Notts), and was educated at Eton. He was a Captain in the 3rd Hussars and a J.P. in West Riding. Barrister-at-Law, Lincoln's Inn 1895.

56

The records show that Jebb played to scratch and his son Henry Cecil Edward, who was born in 1889 and died in 1951, was playing to a handicap of eight in 1904 at the age of 15. A younger son, Alvery Richard Melville, died at the age of nine and a memorial stone can be seen in the garden of Tullich Lodge.

H.S.F. Jebb gifted the Font to St Kentigern's Church. The stone work was by George Hall, Builders, and the cover was carved by Jas. Ogilvie & Sons, Aberdeen.

Kenneth Francis Gordon 1910 to 1911. K.F. Gordon was born in 1877 and he died in 1959. H.S.F. Jebb resigned by letter in August 1909 but the Committee declined to accept it until the A.G.M. held in May 1910. At that meeting K.F. Gordon, the brother of Reginald Hugh Lyall Gordon, the nineteenth Laird of Abergeldie, was elected Captain. Dr A.C. Profeit was in the chair (in the absence of the Captain) and Gordon was proposed by D. Birrell and seconded by W. Willox. He attended a Club meeting on 12th May 1910 and a Committee meeting on 5th July 1910. However he does not appear to have attended any further meetings.

At a meeting held on 9th May 1911 six members, including KFG were to have their handicaps reduced from 4 to Scratch although the higher handicap was to be retained for use when playing at other courses. This decision caused some unrest among members of the Committee who had not been present. The Rev. A. Gerry wrote protesting that the 'said committee' was not properly constituted and so the meeting of 15th May decided that 'all members of the Club be requested to send in three certified scores for handicap between 1st and 15th June'. In October 1912 Gordon presented a prize to be played for in the winter months.

Alexander Charles Profeit 1911 to 1913. M.D., M.B., C.M., Aberdeen. Died 14th January 1934. He was the Club Secretary from July 1908 until May 1909 when John Hanna was appointed. Dr Profeit returned to Ballater after the War and was elected to the Committee at the A.G.M. in 1920 but there is no further word of him.

A.C. Profeit was Medical Officer of Health Glen Muick, Tullich, and Glen Gairn. Civil Surgeon Victoria Hospital and Asst. Medical Officer Fisherton Hospital Asylum. Author 'Army Inefficiency; its Greatest Cause'. He lived in Oakleigh, Albert Road.

John Keiller Greig 1923 to 1931. Born Dundee 1881. Died 1971. Brother-in-Law of Jo Keiller. Educated in Dundee. Prior to Great War worked at the Keiller factory in London. Enlisted in Scottish Horse but in view of business experience was drafted into the management of Munitions factories. Post Great War he continued to work as a Director of Keillers. Later he moved to Ballater (Craggan) to become Factor of Morven Estate. J.K.G. was a prominent sportsman in his day. Apart from being a low handicap golfer he won distinction in the Olympic

Games in 1908 when he took the Silver Medal in Ice Skating. With his cousin Alexander Keiller of Craigendarroch House (sometime called Morven) he took part in the Cresta Run in bobsleigh 'White Heather'.

It was John Keiller Greig who, at the half-yearly general meeting on 22nd October 1925, proposed the Membership Rule which, with a small degree of flexibility of residence within a slightly wider defined area, still operates today.

The proposal was:

That no person be admitted as a member unless belonging to the Parishes of Glenmuick, Tullich, and Glengairn and having a permanent residence in either of these places. The question of residence to be defined by the Secretary or Committee if necessary.

Mr Tytler seconded and the motion was unanimously agreed.

James Will Brockie 1931 to 1939 and 1943 to 1945. Brockie was born in 1887 and lived in Louvain, Golf Road. He was Provost of Ballater from 1933 to 1941. He died in August 1958 aged 71. He married Hannah, older sister of Grace, daughters of James Grant (see above). James Brockie was a schoolteacher but was persuaded to manage James Grant's building business in Ballater when Grant became increasingly pre-occupied with business in Aberdeen. The 17th hole is named Brockie's Pond since it was close to his house.

Brockie tried, on several occasions in the thirties, to make graceful exits from the captaincy but was thwarted each time. At the A.G.M. in 1936 for example, in his farewell speech he said what a happy year it had been whereupon W. Porter who had been proposed as Captain said that he hoped the Captain would accept another year of happiness. And he did!

T.Reid 1939. At the A.G.M. on 29th March 1939 the date clashed with an election meeting and only thirteen members attended. However business got under way and Will Brockie stood his ground—he declined to serve for another year. Four others were proposed in succession but each declined. They were W. Findlay, D.E. Rezin, T. Reid, and the Rev. J. Howat. The meeting then decided that in view of the poor attendance to adjourn the appointment of Captain and other officials to another meeting to be held on Wednesday 12th April.

The adjourned A.G.M. duly took place on 12th April. Only ten members were present when Mr J. Burnett proposed, seconded by Mr D.C. Logan, that Mr T. Reid be appointed Captain. Mr Reid accepted office on the basis that it would be for one year only. D.C. Logan was appointed Vice-Captain.

In the event Mr Reid attended several committee meetings through June but at a meeting on 7th September (one week after the start of the War) a letter was read announcing his resignation. D.C. Logan chaired subsequent meetings until he was elected Captain at the A.G.M. in 1940.

Douglas Campbell Logan 1940 to 1943. D.C. Logan was born on 21st January 1880 at Midmill of Cruden near Hatton, Aberdeenshire. He was one of a family of six (Willie, John, Edith, Hilda, Douglas, and Gordon) and was educated at Robert Gordon's College. He married Marion Ainslie Smith, daughter of Andrew Smith, Factor of the Invercauld Estate. D.C.L. was Factor of Kenmore, Perthshire, Arisaig, Inverness-shire, and at St Andrews, Fife, before becoming tenant of the Royal Hotel, Stonehaven, and finally the tenant of the Invercauld Arms Hotel (and farm), Ballater. He died on 19th June 1958 at Ballater at the age of 78. Logan was the last tenant of the Invercauld Arms—following his death the hotel was sold to Colonel Charles Napier. His son Andrew (Paddy) Logan died on 24th February 1983.

George MacKenzie Rezin 1945 to 1953. Born in Cults, Aberdeen 1907, George Rezin died in February 1953. He was educated in Cults, Banff, Ballater, and at Banchory Academy. A promising career in Banking was short lived when, deciding to get into business on his own account, he bought a newsagent and bookseller shop in Ballater from his sister when she married. He was a talented pianist but played mainly for his own and his family's pleasure. His golf gave pleasure to many. In 1951 Rezin was elected an honorary life member.

D.C. Logan   *George Rezin.*

A committee meeting was held on the evening of the day that George Rezin died and the following appreciation was minuted:

The Ballater Golf Club has suffered a severe loss in the death of the Captain Mr George M. Rezin. Mr Rezin has been a member of the Club since his early youth and has been Captain for the last eight years.

Apart from his outstanding ability as a player, Mr Rezin's work in connection with the running of the Club extended far beyond his duties as Captain. The amount of time he spent on the business of the Club, both financially and technically can only be appreciated by the members who had the good fortune to work with him in committee. His outstanding abilities and unselfishness in Club matters are solely responsible for the Club being in the happy position it is today.

He was the ideal Captain and a great sportsman. His prowess at the game was widely known and he was a popular figure on courses all over the North-east. His personality, good judgement and sound knowledge of everything pertaining to the game will be sadly missed by all his colleagues. His passing at such an early age is an irreparable loss to the whole community.

Dr J.G. Moir 1953 to 1955. James Moir was born in Aberdeen in 1917 and died in Ballater at the age of 68 in September 1985. He was an Aberdeen Grammar School F.P. and graduated M.B., Ch.B. at Aberdeen University in 1939. Dr Moir was a University Tennis Blue and Captain. During World War ll he served with the RAMC in India and Burma.

A.J. Todd 1955 to 1961. In 1956 there was a ballot for the office of Captain. Alex Todd (who owned the Morven Cafe which subsequently became the Coach House) had been proposed by Dr Alan Gibb who was then, himself, proposed by Mr Coutts. The voting resulted in a win for Mr Todd. In the contest for Vice-Captain there were nominations for Tom Forbes, George Smith, and Alan Gibb. The ballot resulted in a very narrow win for Alan Gibb.

Again, in 1957 there was a ballot for the Captaincy and Alex Todd was re-elected.

W.G. Richmond 1961 to 1964. Gordon Richmond was born in Ballater and educated locally until he spent a year at Gordon's College in Aberdeen. He is the senior Past-Captain and as such is joint chairman of the Centenary organising committee.

In 1942 he joined the Army (Signals Corp) subsequently meeting his wife-to-be when serving in Austria. Returning to Ballater in 1947 he purchased a Dry Dairy (Dry because he owned no cows) collecting milk at 4 a.m. from local farms including Balmoral. Eventually he gave this up and worked with an oil company in Aberdeen. His daughter Jane is married to Alan Michie (son of Matt and Rose Michie) the present Vice-Captain. Daughter Elizabeth is unmarried and lives in London, while

60

Striding out at the start of a season in the 1950's are Willie (Bill) Leith, Andrew (Paddy) Logan, George Leith, Alan Gibb, and Alec Todd.

Ingrid is married to Club member Finlay Grant. His son Gordon is married and lives in Dyce.

Gordon's lowest handicap was 7 and his name is to be seen on any number of trophies.

Gordon Richmond's father, who came to Ballater from Glasgow following World War 1, was a Grocer (one of the six in Ballater at that time) with premises at the corner of Golf Road and Dee Street. Richmond owned most of the property round the corner from the store in Dee Street (the portion known as Claikies Brae) and was Dean of Guild in 1951 when the Town Council recommended to Captain Farquharson that he should approve that the golf course should be opened for play from 10 a.m. Later he became Provost (from 1942 to 1947) and his name lives on in Richmond Place, off Deebank Road.

G.J. Smith 1964 to 1967. George Smith was born and educated in Ballater. After school he spent a year at the Commercial College in Aberdeen and then joined up in the Kings Hussars. At his own request he transferred to the 1st Royal Tank Regiment thinking that this would give him an opportunity to drive a tank. However when the authorities learned of his commercial experience he was put into an office. The Smith family owned George Smith & Co. (Fishing Tackle Makers. Salmon flies dressed on the premises. Ammunition and Golfing outfits. Saddlery), in Bridge Street.

The period from 1964 to 1970 was of particular importance in Club affairs. During his time in office George Smith started the negotiations which would lead ultimately to the purchase of the course from the Invercauld Estate. He was also involved in the preparatory work of altering the course and improving the Clubhouse. All these matters were concluded during Harry Wright's Captaincy.

Henry B. Wright 1967 to 1970. Harry Wright was born in York in 1913. He joined the Customs and Excise Service in 1934 and served in the R.A.F. and R.A.F.V.R. from 1941 to 1949 including three years as a flying instructor in Southern Rhodesia. When he retired in 1949 as a Flight/Lieut. he returned to Customs and Excise and was posted to Crathie as the Excise Officer at Lochnagar Distillery. During his Captaincy the Club completed the purchase of the course from the Invercauld Estate. Affectionately known as 'Mr Sweeper', Harry has taken on the work of organising the very popular 'Sweepers' held around midday on Tuesdays, Thursdays, Saturdays, and Sundays throughout the year. At one time close to being a single figure golfer Harry has achieved six holes in one!

He was a founder members of the Crathie Cricket team.

Harry Wright is credited with first suggesting (in 1956) that a practice net be purchased—a suggestion that has been repeated many times!

At a recent End of Season Review meeting when there had been a somewhat tortuous discussion about the positioning of bunker rakes Harry brought the debate to an end by suggesting that players should 'remove the rakes before moving the bunkers'!

M.G.A. Michie 1970 to 1973. Matt was born in 1915 in Killarney, the house in Golf Road where he and Rose live. He was educated in Ballater, joined the Post Office in 1929 and stayed for 45 years (including Army service from 1939 to 1946) before retiring in 1975. In those days the Post Office was located in the Albert Hall, moving to Netherley Place around 1977.

Matt was a Sergeant/Instructor in the Seaforth Highlanders for most of the War and was stationed at Fort George and Elgin.

J.D. Hynd 1973 to 1976. Born 19th June 1910 in Burnley, Lancashire. Educated at Rydal School, Colwyn Bay 1921–1927. He spent three years 'going through the Mill' in his father's cotton weaving factory in Nelson before transferring to the Manchester Sales Office. Joining the Army at the outbreak of war he moved rapidly from square-bashing at Chilwell (Private), near Nottingham, to the R.A.O.C. (2nd Lieut.) and on to the

J.D. Hynd

Persian Gulf where he was promoted Captain and then Major. Hynd's main task in the Middle East was to ensure that all the textile factories in the area were supplied with spare parts so that they could keep their machinery running, thus saving the shipping of finished textiles from the U.K. After the war he organised the establishment of a modern textile plant on the outskirts of Baghdad. This mission completed, came the revolution and back to England where he became Managing Director of a Spinning and Weaving factory in Littleborough. Retirement was initially to Ballater—'Lochnagar'—and then 'Sluie Cottage' before moving to Arran which Donald claims is equally beautiful and certainly warmer.

Ian M. Paterson 1976 to 1979. Born in 1935 and educated in Aboyne, Ian attended the Aberdeen Trades School before serving a five year apprenticeship in Marine Engineering at Hall Russells. He then joined BP Tankers and sailed the seas, sometimes accompanied by his wife, Ballater born Nancy Bruce (Ladies Captain from 1982 to 1983) whom he married in 1958.

Wilfrid Hardman 1979 to 1982. Bill Hardman was born in Bury, Lancashire in 1912. He served 20 years in the Royal Navy from 1933 to 1953, then a further 20 years in the Merchant Navy before retiring in 1973. During his forty years at sea Bill was a Warrant Officer Purser. In

1942 he was captured by the Japanese and held prisoner in Sumatra for three and a half years. It was during this period that he lost the use of an eye through malnutrition. Lady Mountbatten was the first to enter the camp to tell the POWs that the war was over and they were about to be flown out. A former member of the Rangoon Golf Club, Bill and his wife moved with their family (three sons and a daughter) to Ballater in 1961 and became members of the Club and active competitors. Bill admits his handicap never bettered 15. No holes in one.

Rupert Macnamee 1982 to 1984. Rupert Macnamee was born in Edinburgh in 1927 and educated in the City. After University he spent a couple of years in the Navy before joining a Publishing house and then starting his own Publishing enterprise. In the early 1970's he and his eldest son Christopher started an oil related company in Aberdeen and recently they have established an outpost in Houston, Texas.

Some years ago he was persuaded to buy a Sub Post Office in Edinburgh. He added to this by taking over the Ballater Post Office when it was located in the Albert Hall. Later he moved it to Netherley Place.

In the old days in Edinburgh Rupert was Captain of the Northern Merchants and The Edinburgh Merchants Golf Company who played their golf at Bathgate.

John Pringle 1984 to 1986. John Pringle has been Motor Mechanic, Jeweller, spare time footballer, walker and climber, powerful golfer, and recently he has been working for Craigendarroch Ltd. John is Ballater born and bred. He worked for his father at the garage in Victoria Road, before moving to the shop at the corner of Bridge Street and Victoria Road.

Alan Mitchell 1986 to 1989. Alan Mitchell and his wife Helen are Aberdonians. Alan was born in 1946. Since leaving school he has been connected with telephones, at one time in Ballater and now, working for British Telecom, in Aberdeen. He retains his home in Ballater.

Over the years his golf has been somewhat better than average. Under the old handicapping system he was down to three. Nowadays he plays to around ten. His eldest son performed with distinction in the Ballater Open in 1990 and 1991. If there should be a problem with the rules members tend to turn to Alan. He is the master of the rule book and if in doubt he will work it out with a combination of common sense and fairness.

Dr W.G.C. Manson 1989 to 1991. A graduate of Aberdeen University Bill Manson practised in Alford for many years. A 'very-nearly-very-good' golfer with a long, elegant, backswing and a greenside manner that is an example to us all.

R.G. Petrie 1991 to 1993. Bob Petrie comes from Towie where he was educated. He worked for a time in Tarland before moving to Ballater in 1978. He married Gillian Thain in 1982 forming a powerful golf part-

Past Captains—Back row, left to right: John Pringle 1984–1986. Dr W.G.C. Manson 1989–1991. W.G. Richmond 1961–1964. R.G. Petrie 1991–1992. A.A. Mitchell 1986–1989. I.M. Paterson 1976–1979. M.G.A. Michie 1970–1973. Front row: H.B. Wright 1967–1970. W. Hardman 1979–1982. G.J. Smith 1964–1967. R. Macnamee 1982–1984. (J.D. Hynd 1973–1976 now lives on Arran.)

nership. Ask Sandy or Anne Grant who had to play them one summer evening in 1991. The Petries holed out in 67 gross (five threes and two two's) but the gritty Grants won the match at the 19th with a four and the help of a stroke!

HONORARY MEMBERS

John Smart Horse hirer. In 1906 for financial assistance.

Lucien Bertrand Squires Knowles. In April 1922 Major J. Milne asked the Club if it would be willing to grant Life Membership to the winner of a Golden Ballot which was being organised by ex-servicemen to raise money for a recreation hut in Ballater. The Club agreed to this and Mr Knowles was the winner.

James Grant. April 1923. '. . . in appreciation of his service as Captain and member for many years.'

William W. Tytler. April 1927. He gave a loan of £300 to the Club when work on the course extension was under way in 1925/6. In October 1927 he resigned as he was leaving the District. The loan was repaid in April 1929. Mr Tytler had a Chemist shop in Bridge Street.

Robert Stewart November 1927. He had given £10 to the Club at a time when the finances were in poor shape. Stewart had two hairdressing shops in Ballater. (To put this in perspective it should be remembered that £10 was a substantial gift in terms of the value of money at that time. Even twenty years later in the years following the War a wage of £10 per week was earned only by those in the highest skilled jobs such as craftsmen in the Printing or Mining Industries.)

George Rezin 1951. For services as Captain and member of the Club for many years.

A.W. Leonard Club Steward from 1947 to 1955. For past services to the Club.

John Worling August 1958. For services to the Club over twenty years. He lived in Coyle View, Salisbury Road.

Charles Cumming April 1960. For his advice and the work he did in drawing up the plans for laying the tracks for the pipes supplying water to various points on the course. He was the Borough Foreman responsible for the maintenance and supply of all the village services. He would rise at three a.m. in the summer and clear the streets of rubbish to ensure that visitors were presented with a clean village. Cumming was succeeded firstly by Alexander Alexander (known, of course, as Double Sandy!) and then by Sandy Sinclair.

Captain Harold F. Phillips Oakleigh, Albert Road. Proposed by the Vice-Captain H.B. Wright in March 1967, being at that time the Club's oldest golfing member. Captain Phillips married Victoria, daughter of Dr Alexander Profeit of Balmoral and their grandson Victor Jordan still owns the property in Albert Road. Captain Phillips was 100 years old on 30th November 1977.

Mrs Alice Parker was made a Life Member in February 1968. This was in recognition of her life long association with the Club.

Mr R.R. Law. In January 1973 for services to the Club.

Matt Michie. For a life of service to the Golf Club and the community. The Ballater Golf Club's elder statesman.

J. B. RENNETT.
ADVOCATE
AND
CHARTERED ACCOUNTANT.

TELEPHONE No. 486.

231a *Union Street,*

Aberdeen.

4th August 1906.

John Beaton, Esq.,
North of Scotland Bank House,
Ballater.

Dear Mr Beaton,

Ballater Golf Club.

I have received yours of 2nd inst. and although its terms are all too flattering as regards myself I thank the Committee for the kind feelings which prompted the letter and the request contained therein, I need hardly say it will give me the greatest pleasure to be present on the occasion of the Luncheon to be given by Mr Anderson of Oakhall on the 16th inst., but I feel that there will be many persons there far better fitted than I to propose such an important Toast as that of the Ballater Golf Club. At the same time, since the Committee has been kind enough to ask me — an honour which, I assure you, I appreciate very highly — I shall endeavour to do justice to the Toast on the auspicious occasion, unless between now and then someone else occurs to your Committee to whom the Toast should be entrusted, and in that event I hope you will not hesitate to put another in my place, for, as I have said, I shall be very glad to be present without taking any part in the proceedings.

Again thanking the Committee and yourself for thinking of me in this connection,

I am,
Yours very truly,
Barclay Rennett.

67

SEVEN

The Ladies

'Women on the course! They'll be wanting to play next'—the Oldest Member restless in his slumbers.

(With apologies to P.G. Woodhouse)

*　　　　　*　　　　　*

The first mention of Ladies at Ballater:

7th April 1893. It was resolved that the subscription for Ladies be 2/6 for one month or less, or 5/- for the season, or they may join as members. The same terms to apply to boys under 16.

The Ballater Golf Club has accepted from the beginning that the course should be available to all. In the 1990's, however, there are still some restrictions; ladies take no part in the management of the Club and are not considered full members. From time to time proposals have been made to improve the status of the Ladies (e.g. to allow them to be represented at Council meetings) but the opposing forces have always won the day. However, there are signs of a changing mood within the Club and it may not be long before the Constitution is altered.

Since the Ladies are not full members they do not, of course, attend A.G.M.'s. But an inspection of the names of those present at the A.G.M. on 23rd March 1949 reveals that of Alice R. Parker! During the meeting Tom Forbes proposed a vote of thanks to the Ladies for organising the popular Mixed Foursomes and Mrs Parker replied for the Ladies. A very special occasion!

*　　　　　*　　　　　*

68

The Club Council met on 20th January 1914:

A letter from Mrs J. Lumsden regarding the formation of a Ladies Golf Club was read by the Chairman [James Grant]. After discussion the Committee agreed to have the matter brought before the Club A.G.M. in May.

At the A.G.M. following a discussion the Chairman proposed that a Ladies Club be formed. This was agreed unanimously but:

it must be understood by Ladies joining that they had no powers in the management of the Club outside their own section; and that only those residing in the District are eligible for membership.

At a meeting following the A.G.M. it was agreed that members of the Club joining the Ladies section would pay a subscription of 7/6 annually.

The War intervened and there is no further mention of a Ladies Section until the A.G.M. of 1930:

Ladies Club. Colonel Stewart proposed that the Lady Members be invited to form a Ladies Golf Club. Mr W. Rowell seconded. Agreed unanimously.

There is no mention of the fees to be charged although in 1914 the Council had agreed that the Ladies would pay substantially less than the men.

The Minute Book of the Ladies section records:

A General Meeting was held in the Golf Pavilion on Thursday 15th May 1930 at 8 p.m. to discuss the formation of a Ladies Section. Mr Keiller Greig presided. Those present were: Misses Meg Watt, May Grant, Betty Knowles, Winnie Leith, A. Scott, Tibbie Grant, Maxwell, Carnegie, Mrs Parker, and Mrs Rowell, all of whom approved of such a move. Office bearers were then elected.

Captain: *Grace Grant*   Vice-Captain: *Alice Parker*
Joint Secretaries: *Miss Scott* and *Margaret (Meg) Watt*
Committee: *May Grant, Jean Watt*, and *Mrs Rowell*

THE LADY CAPTAINS

Grace Grant 1930 to 1932. Gracie Grant, the younger daughter of James Grant former Captain of the Club and Provost of Ballater became the first Captain of the Ladies Section. Unmarried, she lived with her sister Hannah (Nan) and her brother-in-law J.W. Brockie (who in turn became Club Captain and Provost of Ballater). When her brother Joseph was appointed to the charge of Rhynie Church in 1933 she became his housekeeper until he joined the Army in 1940 and subsequently married. Thereafter Grace lived in Moorfield (one of the family

This photograph was probably taken in the late 1920's.
Back row: Left to right. ?. W. (Windy) Watt, Farmer at Mill of Prony. ?.
James Low of Clydesdale Bank. A.D. McHardy, Kettledrum restaurant, Bridge
Street. Tibbie Grant, Boarding House keeper (now Post House). Daisy Harper,
helped her father who had the fish shop in Bridge Street (now the greengrocer).
Essel Rezin, sister of George Rezin. She married Ronnie Middleton, a Glen
Muick gamekeeper and they emigrated to New Zealand.
Middle Row: Alice Parker, married an Australian. Miss Souper, Davidson
and Smith, Bridge Street. Meg Watt, sister of W. Watt. J. Findlay, taxidermist.
John Lumsden with cup, Vice-Captain 1913–1928 (Lumsden & Gibson?). D.N.
Chisholm the Headmaster. Christian Lumsden, daughter of John Lumsden. Grace
Grant, first Ladies Captain. Winnie (Leith) Davidson, daughter of George Leith
the Baker.
Front row: George Ironside the woodwork teacher. Ian Findlay, son of John
Findlay, teacher at Dalry, Ayrshire. John Milne, a Grocer in Bridge Street (now
T.S.B.). Jo Grant. George Rezin. Dr Levack?
In a letter from Spondon dated June 1991 Daisy Harper (now Mrs Christie)
admits a memory problem but thinks that the bottom right man 'was the
Postmaster, a friend of the Watts of Prony'. She also thinks that the unidentified
man top left 'was the son of a baker who had the shop opposite the present Co-op
. . . and that the man to the right of W. Watt was a bank clerk'. Daisy goes on to
say that her father had two shops in Ballater and one in Braemar which she
managed for ten summers.

houses), until moving to sheltered accommodation in Bellfield, Banchory, in 1987.

Jane Watt 1932 to 1937. Jane was the daughter of the Minister at Gairnside in Glen Gairn. They lived in the Manse near the Church until he retired. They then moved to 'Stanmore' in Queens Road.

Isabella R. Urquhart 1937 to 1939. Miss Urquhart was an infant school teacher.

Miss Isabella Wilson 1939. Miss Wilson lived at The Beeches, (now Gairn Lodge) Golf Road and later in Dee Street. At one time she worked as a secretary at the saw mill just outside Ballater on the main road east, close to Aberdeen House.

The second World War now intervened. No further committee meetings were held until 1948 when, on 11th February, the Ladies Section met in the Albert Hall with George M. Rezin (Captain) and Norman Thain present.

Miss Wilson opened the meeting by explaining that as the Ladies Captain in 1939 she had been approached by the Golf Club to call a meeting with the object of reviving the Ladies Club. She then called on George Rezin who said the Club Council at a recent meeting had suggested that they would be glad to see the Ladies Section active again. . . .

The Ladies then appointed officers.

Alice R. Parker 1948 to 1950. She was a keen participant in the Ballater Amateur Dramatic group. Her sister, Jean Calder, became a stewardess with the P & O Line.

Ella Robertson 1950 to 1951. And 1956. Born in Banchory. Wife of Alan Robertson, (see the Riverside Trophy). Some years ago the *Piper* printed:

ELLA IS ON THE BALL . . .

Keen golfer Mrs Ella Robertson, who is in her seventies, proves that age is no obstacle.

For the member of Ballater Golf Club has not only organised winter golf for the local ladies, but also managed to play more than fifty times during the winter season—in all weathers!

During the Fifties and Sixties when there were not many more than a dozen lady golfers playing with any frequency, Ella, Peggy Sutherland, and Rose Michie were known as the three musketeers because of their enthusiasm for striding out in all weathers to do battle with the course!

Betty Frai 1951 to 1954. Wife of Captain Frai, daughter of Gracie Fenton of the well known Edinburgh Jewellery store.

Joyce E.M. McHardy 1954 to 1956. At the A.G.M. in February Stella Leith was appointed Captain but shortly afterwards she said that she couldn't accept office and at a special meeting in June Joyce McHardy was elected. Her father owned the Kettledrum Restuarant.

Rose Michie 1957 to 1973. Rose was born in the bedroom behind the dormer window on the top left of the roof of Aultonrea, the house in Glen Muick featured in 'The Roup' painted by Howard Butterworth. The print can be seen in many houses locally.

Rose (Mitchell) was educated in the school in Glen Muick and then at Crathie. She and Matt were married at Crathie Church in 1939, the Balmoral Girl Guides (of which Rose had been a Captain) providing the Guard of Honour.

Anne Grant 1973 to 1977. Aberdeen born wife of gritty Ballater golfer Alex (Sandy) Grant. Anne was a pupil of Jock Lawson who used to come over from Murcar and in his time taught many of the Ballater youngsters.

Sandy (who has had a single figure handicap for many, many years) and Anne are a formidable partnership. Together (with Sandy the Manager) they make shopping at Strachan's Ballater store a happy experience.

Peggy Sutherland 1977 to 1979. Peggy, wife of Stuart Sutherland, came from Tarves. Stuart was from Portsoy. He was in the Merchant Navy during the War and after working in Aboyne he set himself up as a Painter and Decorator in Ballater.

Betty Simpson 1979 to 1981. Betty Simpson was born in Aberdeen but lived in Ballater from the age of two and was educated in the village and at Banchory Academy. She is the wife of Ian Simpson who has won the Club Championship twice. Before the arrival of two daughters she was a frequent evening golfer and moderate player (nine handicap). Nowadays she is a part-time secretary at the Surgery, and is secretary of the Ballater Amenities Committee which ensures that the Christmas dinner and entertainment for Pensioners continues, as it has, for many years. She is also secretary of the Medical Amenities Fund, and is an Elder of the Glen Muick Church.

Betty Simpson was the Golf Club Secretary from 1968 to 1975.

Rosalind Roy 1981. Rosalind comes from Aboyne, was educated in the north-east, and has been a skilful golfer (low handicap of five) for some years. She was a Scottish Selector from 1984 to 1986, and has played for the Aberdeenshire County Ladies. In 1971 Rosalind held the course record, 71, for six months.

Nancy Paterson 1982 to 1983. Nancy is the wife of Ian Paterson who was Club Captain from 1976 to 1979. She is Ballater born, took up golf later than most and has become a most enthusiastic golfer.

Molly Godsman 1983 to 1985. English by birth Molly spent more years in Aberdeen than anywhere else. Her father was in 'fish' (as they say) and the family moved from east coast England to the north-east of Scotland. She and her husband David moved to Ballater when he retired

72

Top: Ernest Murray, surrounded by competitors, hands the Ballater Open trophy to Nancy Duncan of Brechin. Lesley Grant is behind Rose Michie. Other well known Ballater members include Ella Robertson (front left) and Betty Simpson.
Bottom: Janette Wright receives the Open trophy from Alice Parker. Evelyn Greig, Edith Stuart, and Sheena King are among the prize winners in front.

from the Bank. She continues to hit a mean ball down the middle—a requirement in foursomes in which she excels.

In 1979 Molly was Captain of the North of Scotland Veteran Golfing Association.

Margaret Cassie 1985 to 1988. Daughter of a Dinnet gamekeeper. She and her husband (Alister) run the best hardware store in these parts. It's in Bridge Street.

Eileen Macnamee 1988 to 1990. Eileen hails from Leith. She and Rupert are another formidable foursomes partnership.

Margaret Joss 1990 to 1992. The Centenary Year Lady Captain. Born and brought up in Banchory, Margaret was taught by Tom MacNaughton, the Professional at the Banchory Club, after the last war. Her husband Douglas, who was Manager of the Clydesdale Bank in Alford, retired recently.

Margaret won the Scottish Veteran's Championship in 1986 and has represented Scotland four times in the International Veterans Jamborees. She has also played for Aberdeenshire County Ladies.

THE CHALLENGE CUP

The Ladies Section Minute Book records the proceedings of a meeting held on 1st September 1930:

> A letter was read by the Secretary from Mr Cecil A. Munro, secretary of the Ballater Golfers' Dance asking the [Ladies] to accept a cup and Miniature to the value of the proceeds of the dance. The offer was accepted.... The Captain intimated her intention of gifting a prize to the Club which, together with a prize gifted by Mr William Fraser, Jeweller, ... should be played for simultaneously with the Cup match.... It was unanimously decided that the Cup be won on a scratch score, while the two other prizes be won on handicap scores, both on double rounds.

This is the Ladies Championship and is played over two rounds, a week apart, in June. The board in the Clubhouse records the names of the winners since the competition started in 1930 but the earliest record of scores is 1979.

Grace Grant 1930 Ladies Captain. Handicap 22.

Christian Lumsden 1931. Daughter of John Lumsden who was Vice-Captain of the Club from 1913 to 1928. Handicap 21.

Alice R. Parker 1932, 1948, 1950.

Audrey M. Miller 1933.

Jane F. Watt 1934, 1935, 1936. Winner in three of her six years as Captain.

Winifred Leith (Davidson) 1937. Mother of Roger and Angus.

Alice R. Parker 1938.

74

1989 The Challenge Cup. From the left: Sheena Gordon (3rd), Heather Backhouse (2nd), and Margaret Joss, the Champion. The handicap winners (continuing from the left) were Ella Stewart 1st, Susan Lawson 2nd, Eileen Foggie 3rd, and Muriel Fedo 4th.

Rose Christie 1949, 1962. Rose was the wife of Ed Christie, the greenkeeper/professional.

Betty Frai 1951, 1952, 1953.

Mrs A. Robertson 1954, 1955, 1957, 1959, 1960, 1961, 1965, 1971.

Mrs E. Sutherland 1956, 1958, 1963, 1964, 1966, 1967, 1969, 1970, 1972. Apart from 1962 (Rose Christie) and 1968 (Rose Michie) Ella Robertson and Peggy Sutherland dominated the eighteen years from 1954 to 1972.

Rose Michie 1968. Ladies Captain.

Anne Grant 1973. After a play-off with Peggy Sutherland.

Rosalind Roy 1974, 1975, 1976, 1978.

Molly Godsman 1977.

Gillian Thain 1979, 1980, 1981, 1982.

75

Gillian Petrie 1983, 1985, 1988, 1991.

Gillian's lowest handicap, so far, has been three. She has played for the Scottish Universities (M.A. Aberdeen) in Wales and Eire, and for the Scottish School Girls and Aberdeenshire.

In 1978 Gillian (Thain) Petrie and Pamela Wright of Aboyne were the Scottish Finalists in the Aer Lingus final in Ireland.

Gillian had the best possible teacher—her father Norman Thain. She holds the course record of 69 scored in the September 1990 medal.

Gillian's aggregate scores in the championship have been: *1980*—160. *1981*—166. *1982*—155. *1983*—163. *1985*—146. *1988*—158. *1991*—149.

Sarah MacLennan 1984, 1986, 1987. Sarah, having reached scratch, the lowest handicap ever for a lady golfer in Ballater, turned professional in 1988 and is now to be found at the East Sussex National where she is assistant professional. There is no need of a slow motion replay when taking a look at Sarah's swing—it is slow, smooth and elegant.

Sarah's scores have been: *1984*—146. *1986*—155. *1987*—150. In 1984 her score included 71 in the second round.

Margaret Joss 1989. With an aggregate of 158.

Sheena Gordon 1990. With an aggregate of 149.

Around the mid-seventies the standard of play in the Ladies section began to improve significantly as a younger school of golfers emerged. There are more members and there is much more competition. Molly Godsman readily admits that winning the Challenge Cup in 1977 was no great feat since she won with two scores in the eighties. Nowadays two scores in the seventies are often required and the ladies who have produced these low scores are Sarah MacLennan, Gillian Petrie, Margaret Joss, Sheena Gordon, and Ros Roy. A non-winner, Heather Backhouse, whose handicap came down steadily through the eighties (18 to 5) came close to winning the Challenge Cup in 1988 (3rd), 1989 (2nd) and 1990 (2nd).

*　　　　　*　　　　　*

The WPGA with Carlsburg as sponsors held a 36 hole tournament at Ballater on 14th and 15th June 1979. Beverly Huke won with 146. Local golfers who were invited to compete with the professionals included Gillian Petrie who scored 79 84 for a total of 163, Pam Wright who is competing successfully in the professional field in the USA scored two 81's for 162, Catriona Hardman daughter of former Captain Bill Hardman, and Stella Bruce, at that time playing out of Aberdeen Ladies and now a member at Ballater.

*　　　　　*　　　　　*

THE GLENMUICK SCRATCH CHALLENGE TROPHY

The Ballater Ladies Open Tournament

1953 Mrs J.L. Williams. 80. Aberdeen Ladies Ladies Golf Club and County Captain.

1954 Miss C. Lyon. 81. In 1956 Miss (Lottie) Lyon, after 35 years as Honorary Secretary, was elected the first Honorary Life Member of the Aberdeen Ladies' Golf Club. A month later The Royal Aberdeen Golf Club gave her the courtesy of the courses for life. She retired in 1972 having served as secretary for 51 years. A Vice-President of the Scottish Ladies Golf Association.

1955 Miss Jean Pelham Burn. 77. Perthshire County player from Pitlochry.

1956 Miss L.D. Grant. 78. Banchory Golf Club. Banchory Champion many times. Played for Aberdeenshire.

1957 Miss A.V. Laing. 79. Aberdeen Ladies G.C. Scottish Ladies Golf Champion in 1970 when she beat Belle Robertson at Dunbar. A Scottish Captain.

1958 Mrs J.P. Kennaway. 80. Aberdeen Ladies and Deeside. County player.

1959 Miss A.V. Laing. 77. Winner for the second time.

1960 Mrs J.N. Aitken. 77. Murcar. Past County Captain.

1961 Mrs I. Wright. 74. Janette (Robertson) Wright represented Britain in the Curtis Cup in 1954, 1956, 1958, and 1960. She was Scottish Lady champion four times and Scottish team captain three times. She and her husband Innes Wright (the Aboyne professional) are Honorary Members of the Aboyne Golf Club.

1962 Miss J.L. Brown. 78. Peterhead and Aberdeen Ladies. Played for Aberdeenshire.

1963 Mrs E. Foggie. 78. A powerful golfer, Eileen Foggie was the first member to win the Ballater Open.

1964 Mrs W.R. Wisely. 76. Aberdeen Ladies.

1965 Miss K.L. Lackie. 75. Montrose Royal Albert. Now Mrs Copley and 1991 Chairman of the S.L.G.A.

1966 Mrs I. Wright. 74. For the second time.

1967 Miss N. Duncan. 77. Brechin. Captain Angus and Scottish selector.

1968 Miss A.V. Laing. 75. For the third time.

1969 Miss N. Duncan. 74. For then second time.

1970 Mrs I. Wright. 74. For the third time.

1971 Miss N. Duncan. 78. For the third time.

1972 Miss K.L. Lackie. 71. For the second time.

1973 Miss K.L. Lackie. 73. For the third time.

1974 Miss M.N. Thomson. 70. Muriel Thomson played her first golf at Aboyne and went on to play for Scotland and for Britain in the Curtis Cup in 1978. When she won at Ballater she was a member of Murcar Golf Club. She is now the professional at Portlethen.

1975 Miss Carol Stewart. 74. Many times champion at Murcar. Regular on the Aberdeenshire team.

1976 Miss D.C. Andrew. 73. Gullane. Past Captain East Lothian.

1977 Mrs D.B. Bruce. 74. Formerly Peterhead. Now Aberdeen Ladies and Ballater. Member of the organising committee for the Centenary of Aberdeen Ladies G. C. in 1992. County Captain 1990 and 1991. Past Captain Scottish Veterans.

1978 Miss C.A. Stewart. 71. For the second time.

1979 Mrs J.N. Self. 74. U.S.A. Cruden Bay and Aberdeen Ladies.

1980 Miss C.J. Middleton 79. Formerly of Cruden Bay, now St Rule, one of the Ladies Club in St Andrews. Well-known north-east golfer from a well-known golfing family. Past County Champion.

1981 Miss C.J. Middleton. 72. For the second time.

1982 Miss P. Wright. 68. The record score for the event and a course record at the time. Daughter of Innes and Janette Wright. Now doing well on American circuit as a professional.

1983 Miss P. Wright. 74. For the second time.

1984 Mrs E. Cruickshank. 74. Cruden Bay Golf Club.

1985 Miss Sheena Wood. 75. Well known golfer from Hazlehead. Has played for North of Scotland.

1986 Miss S.N. MacLennan. 76. Ballater. Originally from Edinburgh with considerable golfing background, Sarah turned professional in 1988 and is now to be found at the East Sussex National.

1987 Miss L.A. Urquhart. 73. Banchory. Another well known, talented north-east golfer.

1988 Miss C.J. Middleton. 74. Winner for the third time.

1989 Miss L.A. Urquhart. 73. Winner for the second time.

1990 Miss L.A. Urquhart. 70. Winner for the third time.

1991 Miss C.J. Middleton. 71. Winner for the fourth time.

OTHER TROPHIES

Captain's Cup. 18 holes stableford. Presented by Betty Simpson in 1980.

Corrienearn Trophy. 18 holes stroke play, leading 16 qualify for match play.

Craigard Cup. 36 holes stableford. Presented by Roger Cordiner.

Duncan Trophy Senior Ladies, match play. Presented in 1977 by Mr and Mrs Duncan who used to holiday in Ballater.

Gillies Trophy. 18 holes bogey. Presented by Lewis Gillies in 1962.

Gracie Fenton Cup. Match play. Presented by Mrs Frai in memory of her mother.

Hydro Cup. Ladies/Juniors. 18 holes stroke play. Presented in 1977.

Killarney Trophy. 18 holes, two ball foursomes. Presented by Matt and Rose Michie in 1974.

Golf Week Trophy. Presented in 1976. 18 holes greensomes.

Ladies Match play Trophy. Foursomes. Presented by Rosalind Roy in 1982.

Newlands Rosebowl. 18 holes stroke play. Presented by Mr and Mrs Newlands of Fife.

One-Armed Golfers Trophy. 18 holes strokeplay. Presented in 1976.

Summer Eclectic Trophy. Presented by Mrs Sheila Streatfield at the time of her Golden Wedding in 1984.

Cassie Cup 2×nine holes (over seventies) stableford. Presented by Margaret Cassie in 1989.

Rosebank Trophy. Presented by Ian and Nancy Paterson. The best four rounds of the winter Sundays.

Lady Captains. Rear: Rose Michie, Margaret Cassie, Anne Grant, Nancy Paterson, Rosalind Roy. Front: Eileen Macnamee, Margaret Joss, Ella Robertson, Molly Godsman.

EIGHT

Wigs on the Green

THE BATTLE FOR SUNDAY GOLF

During the Twenties there was a great deal of discussion about the playing of golf on Sundays. At Ballater the first official mention of the subject is contained in a minute of the A.G.M. of 26th April 1928:

> *Sunday play* — Agreed that a general meeting of the Club be called . . . to bring forward the question of having the clauses in the Lease with reference to Sunday golf deleted.

The meeting was held on 9th August with 24 members present. The voting was 14 for and 10 against the motion:

> That this General Meeting of the Ballater Golf Club being of opinion that it will be to the benefit of the Club and the District that facilities for the playing of golf on Sundays would be appreciated, resolve to request Colonel Farquharson of Invercauld to agree to an amendment of the Lease accordingly.

A counter proposal was defeated. The Council met afterwards and a letter signed by 45 visitors protesting against the playing of golf on Sundays was read. The Council decided to acknowledge the letter but take no other action on it.

At the half year meeting held on 18th October a letter which had been received from the Invercauld Factor was read:

> . . . the request of the Club to alter the clause in the Lease prohibiting the playing of golf on Sunday had been submitted to Colonel Farquharson, but owing to several petitions in opposition to the course being open on Sundays, Colonel Farquharson did not feel justified in granting [it] . . .

There is no further reference to the matter until two years later when W. Rowell wrote to the Council suggesting that they get a move on. At

80

the A.G.M. held on 30th April 1931 it was decided to call another Special Meeting of the members.

The meeting was called for 4th June but as only 15 members turned up it was postponed until 10th June when 30 members attended. Mr Rowell proposed the motion, George Rezin seconding, that Colonel Farquharson be asked to delete the clause. The opposition withdrew when it was agreed that play would not start before 2 p.m. The Council decided to write to the Laird.

On 8th July a further general meeting was held to discuss a letter from the Factor stating that the clause relating to Sunday play had been deleted. A motion that the Club adopt Sunday golf from 2 p.m. until dusk on Sundays was adopted and it was agreed that the course would be open for Sunday golf from 12th June 1931, although three and four ball matches were prohibited.

Matters stayed this way until 1945 when, following an exchange of letters with the Estate, it was agreed that the Bowlers could also enjoy their game but, as with the golfers, not before 2 p.m. Thus Sunday mornings were available for worship—but not for long!

At the half year meeting held in November 1948 the first cracks appear. There had been cases of players starting before 2 p.m. and a reminder notice is to be displayed.

Two years later, after reflection and debate within the community, a proposal is made at the half year meeting that the course be open all day on Sundays for play.

The ground had been prepared on both sides—the Chairman, G.M. Rezin, read a letter from the Session Clerk of the Glenmuick Church:

On behalf of the Kirk Session I am instructed to lodge a most emphatic protest against any proposal which will permit of play during the hours of the morning service or say before 1 p.m.

Comments being invited, the Rev. Mr Melville King said he spoke not only for the Presbyterian community but for the Episcopal and Catholic faiths as well. He had unfortunately left at home a letter from the Provost Rev. Canon Adam adding to the protest but he would send it to the Secretary in due course. He said that the Kirk Session had no complaints regarding the playing of golf during the hours obtaining at present or even from 1 o'clock but they could not countenance play during the hours of morning service—Ballater must do what it could to preserve the sanctity of the Scottish Sabbath.

The matter was then put to the meeting and the members voted decisively in favour of Sunday play—26 for the motion, 2 against. The Secretary was to write to the Laird informing him of the result of the meeting. Mr King informed the meeting that he would do all in his power to combat the proposal and asked that the letters from the Ses-

sion Clerk and Provost Adam be put before Captain Farquharson.
Following this decisive vote there was *Press* comment:

SUNDAY GOLF ARGUMENT

The wigs are on the green in Ballater over the Sunday golf question!
Provost Adam himself, the town's Episcopal minister, has led the opposition to the plan to start Sunday golf at 10 a.m. instead of 2 p.m.

With some heat he told me today: 'I think it is a totally unnecessary
step'. He has written to the Laird, Captain Farquharson of Invercauld,
about it.

I should not like to have Capt. Farquharson's responsibility. The golf
club is sending a deputation to request a change in the lease granted by his
grandfather, which governs the hours of Sunday golf ... the ministers in
the town are against it, supported by many churchgoers. His decision is
bound to displease somebody.

Supporters of the golf club point to the overwhelming vote in favour of
the proposal at this week's meeting, and are confident they will have their
way. They say that the opposition of the kirk was inevitable but claim that
only a minority of die-hards support Provost Adam.

Perhaps the town should solve the Sunday question in the House of
Commons way, by a free vote. This would ... take a load off Captain
Farquharson's mind.

A deputation consisting of G.M. Rezin (Capt), Dr J.G. Moir (V-Capt),
A.J. Todd, W. Logan, and the Secretary, met Captain Farquharson in
the Invercauld (now Monaltrie) Hotel on 18th December 1950. The
Laird had been briefed by both parties in the dispute. The Club's point
of view was re-stated—improvement of attraction to visitors, financial
gain not only to the Club but to Ballater as a whole, and little or no harm
done—certainly none to Church attendance. The Laird said he would
consider the matter and advise the Club of his findings.

Captain Farquharson referred the matter to the Town Council and
the following is extracted from the minutes of the meeting held on 12th
February 1951:

Sederunt: Provost Adam. Baillies Smith and Craig. Dean of Guild Richmond. Councillors Begg, Cook, Davidson, Maitland, Paton, and Cook.

Provost Adam was the Rector of St Kentigerns, Baillie Smith of Davidson and Smith (Milliners, Drapery, and Grocer) in Bridge Street, Baillie
Jack Craig was the Headmaster at the School, Dean of Guild Richmond
had the Grocers at the corner of Golf Road and 'Sklakies Brae', and of
the Councillors, Begg had the Boarding House, Morvada, Cook was a
secretary at Strachans Bus Depot, Scott Davidson was of Davidsons the
butchers in Bridge Street (now H.M. Sheridan), Maitland was a Painter
and Decorator, and Paton was the manager of the Co-op Bakery.

After a full discussion it was unanimously decided that a vote should be taken. Dean of Guild Richmond seconded by Bailie T.C. Smith, moved that the vote be taken by ballot. Councillor Begg, seconded by Councillor Davidson moved an amendment that the vote be taken by a show of hands. Four votes were cast for the motion and four for the amendment, there being one abstention, and Provost Adam gave the casting vote in favour of the motion. Thereafter a ballot was held and the Council decided by 7 votes to 2 to recommend to Captain Farquharson that he should approve that the Ballater Golf Course should be open for play on Sundays from 10 a.m.

And so it came to be. But exactly when 10 a.m. became dawn (or even earlier!) is lost in some early morning mist!

*   *   *

The photograph below shows William Porter (Vice-Captain) driving the first Sunday ball. His father was James Porter, the gardener at Monaltrie. Born around 1890, he died in 1975. He had a distinguished career in World War l serving in the Gordon Highlanders and the Royal Flying Corp. His decorations included the Croix de Guerre. In World War ll he joined up and served as a Pilot Officer in the R.A.F. It is said that in order to hide his frequent golfing excursions he played under an assumed name. Its a good story but his employer probably knew all about it! Paddy worked for the Pru.

Sunday Golf at Ballater, in spite of the weather. Mr W. Porter, vice-captain, driving the first ball in the first Sunday match.

NINE

The Club Championship

I n April 1929 at the A.G.M. Mr W. Porter proposed that 'a club championship competition be held once a year in August. It was agreed to leave the matter to the committee to arrange'.

The 1953 A.G.M. was held on 16th March in the Invercauld Arms Hotel. Dr J.G. Moir was elected Captain in succession to George Rezin. Following the A.G.M. the new Captain and the Committee held a meeting and decided that the Summer Competition would in future be called the Club Championship and be played over four rounds. The winner would be the player who had the lowest gross score. Prior to this the winner of the Summer Competition was the player with the lowest net score. The last four winners of the Summer Competition were:

1949	George Leith	(7)	281	Gross	G.M. Rezin	299
1950	Tom Forbes	(5)	282	Gross	Tom Forbes	302
1951	J. Clark	(14)	266	Gross	N. Thain	300
1952	M. Michie	(15)	278	Gross	N. Thain	312

The winners of the Club Championship have all been fine golfers but it is difficult to dispute the view that George Rezin in the Thirties and Forties was in a class of his own. On the Ballater course he was almost unbeatable. It is true that outwith Ballater there is little to judge him by for he seldom took part in other competitions in the area. This was the nature of the man—he devoted himself almost entirely to his local business and the Golf Club. But his record in Club competitions was outstanding and his performances in the Ballater Open in the Thirties almost unbelievable.

George Rezin's best round was recorded in the *Press and Journal* and is clipped into the competition book of the time. This states that in a day in July 1937 he was out in 31, back in 32 for 63. He had nine threes and nine fours. His partners were G. Leith, G.H. Ironside, and James Morrison.

In those days the cream of the north-east golfers came to Ballater to compete in the prestigious competition. Rezin never competed in the (new) Club Championship but it is as certain as anything can be that had he lived he would have won this championship more that once in the Fifties if not in the Sixties. George Rezin was not a Ballater man and it is when we seek to find the best of these that we get into difficulties — as the championship unrolls over the years the candidates will emerge.

Norman Thain

1953	79–75–75–80–309	2nd	Tom Forbes	315
1955	75–76–75–73–299	,,	G. Leith	313
1959	79–76–71–75–301	,,	G.J. Smith	306

Norman Thain was born in Aberdeen in 1920 but moved to Ballater as a child. He was educated at the local school under the very stern (and, some say, much disliked) headmaster D.N. Chisholm. In the thirties he picked up some pennies caddying, attending to the putting green, and odd jobbing in Collies shop. Along with other youngsters he was allowed to potter about the golf course under the watchful eye of John Hanna whose wrath would be great if they didn't clear off on hearing his piercing whistle! Norman was in the Royal Air Force from 1940 to 1946 and on returning to Ballater completed his apprenticeship as a mechanic at the Riverside Garage under Lewis Gillies and, after the war, with Alan Robertson who now owned it. The business was purchased by George Beaton in 1972 and Norman retired in 1985 at the age of 65.

He was on the Club Council for five years from 1947 to 1952. Together with George Rezin he helped to organise the first Open at nearby Braemar, the highest 18 hole course in the U.K.

During the Fifties Norman Thain was clearly a very fine, consistant golfer. Apart from his three championship wins he had returned the best gross scores in the old Summer Competition in 1951 and 1952 and he was runner up in the Championship (to Ian Clark) twice. He didn't play in the Championship in 1960 or 1961 and had some indifferent performances before coming back in 1967 to be runner up to Alistair McGregor.

I.D.R. Clark

1954	78–72–77–72–299	2nd	N. Thain	304
1957	72–74–74–86–306	,,	E. Christie	321
1958	76–75–71–72–294	,,	N. Thain	313

Born in Ballater in 1934 Ian followed in his father's footsteps as a baker. He was apprenticed at the SCWS Bakery in Ballater and worked in the town (apart from 1955 and 1956 when he was serving in the

R.A.F.) before moving to Turriff in 1959, where he won the championship in 1959, 1965 and 1969, and then, finally to Aberdeen in 1974.

He learnt his golf on the Ballater course, much of it caddying for his hero George Rezin. He was very long off the tee but his greatest strength was his ability to hole out in one from anywhere on the green! Many considered 'happy go lucky' Ian to have been the best putter ever seen! 'A round of golf shouldn't need more than twenty putts' he used to say and ask him (as directed) about his favourite putt he says 'downhill and fast'!

Ivor Phillips recalls the 1971 Open at Braemar. He arrived to find Ian Clark, who was about to tee off, jumping up and down wanting him to have a look at his swing which had been letting him down in recent rounds. Ivor took a look and made an adjustment to Ian's take away at address and off he went on his round. The card recording Ian's 59 that day is shown on page 108. His partner was Ian Creswell who returned an almost equally remarkable score of 60. Alistair McGregor remembers the day. Out on the course they could hear the cheers as crowds gathered when word got round that there was something on! Some of Ian's magic has gone nowadays but he still plays to single figures at Hazlehead.

No explanation has been offered for Ian's fourth round of 86 in 1957 but note that he won by 15 shots!

In 1958 no other player scored under 300. Around this time the Club forwarded Ian Clark's name to the North-east District for consideration for selection for inter-district matches.

The Bon-Accord Golf Club of Aberdeen celebrated its Centenary in 1972. Part of the celebrations was a Pro-Am which included, in each team of three, the Champion from 28 north-east Clubs. I.D.R. Clark had won the Bon-Accord Championship in 1971 and the programme notes had this to say about Clark:

Ian won the Bon-Accord Championship at his first attempt. Has won the Turriff and Ballater Championships several times. The highlight last season was an incredible record 59 at Braemar.

Norman McLeod recalls the times when Ernie Murray used to accompany Ian and himself on a round. Those were the days when they bet substantial amounts on the match. On one occasion at the 18th, with the game all square, Norman's drive was on the green while Ian's was in the bushes to the left, some fifty or sixty yards from the green. Murray was a happy man—his money was on McLeod and he left Clark in the bushes wondering how he was going to hole the shot. Eventually the ball emerged from the bushes and disappeared into the hole—just as Ian had planned! McLeod failed to get the half and Murray was left with a scowl on his normally cheerful face!

86

I.G.K. Phillips

| 1956 | 78–75–77–78–308 | 2nd | G. Knowles | 310 |

Ian George Knox Phillips is the eldest of the three sons of the late Aberdeen Fish Merchant, Jocky Phillips. All three were educated at The Aberdeen Grammar School. From there newspaper reporter Ian progressed to a shop in Alford, back to teacher training at the University and then to teaching at Arbroath and Aberdeen.

He was a member of the Club for about ten years having joined at a time when the Club was not imposing residential qualifications.

He and his brothers hold an unusual record in that they were champions of their respective clubs at the same time—Deeside, Hazlehead, and Victoria. At one time they had a combined handicap of three—one was scratch (Ian), one was 1, and the other was 2.

Ian played in the Open Championship at St Andrews in 1964 (Lema's year). Others from the north-east in that Open included Sandy Pirie, J.H. Little, Jack Pressley, Innes Wright, and M.J. Moir.

In 1965, a scratch player at Deeside, he broke the course record there with 67 in the first round of the championship.

Norman McLeod

| 1960 | 78–73–70–70–291 | 2nd | R.A. McGregor | 305 |

When railway services between Aberdeen and Ballater were discontinued in 1966, the last train (the 8.35 p.m. on Saturday 26th February) from Aberdeen was driven by Norman McLeod. Not long retired he now lives in Balloch, at the southern end of Loch Lomond.

Norman was born in Elgin in 1927 and educated at the Bishopmill School and Elgin Academy. He married one of the 'Tomnakeist' Michies.

He writes:

> I was proud to have won the Club Championship that year but like all the Ballater members was sad at the absence of Norman Thain due to illness. It was the first time he had missed the event since I started taking part. After all he was the player I considered you had to beat to win. When I pointed out later to him that it was easy, since he wasn't playing, he quickly pointed out that I had won with the lowest championship score for the four rounds. A great compliment from one of the most consistant golfers I have ever played with. His record proves it.

Norman was also a very consistant golfer since he came second or third in the Championship in the sixties until the end of the railway led to his transfer elsewhere. The sense of humour of some of his friends was put to the test when, in the railway days, as the engine drew level with the 8th green at Aboyne he would sound two blasts on the whistle, timing them to coincide with the backswing of the putter!

R.A. McGregor

1961	75–71–70–68–284	2nd	J.B. Illingworth	307
1962	75–74–77–69–295	,,	E. Christie	305
1963	75–75–70–67–287	,,	J.B. Illingworth	296
1964	70–70–75–69–284	,,	N. McLeod	294
1965	72–76–75–72–295	,,	N. McLeod	309
1966	72–70–71–71–284	,,	G.J. Smith	319
1967	70–72–69–71–282	,,	N. Thain	326
1969	75–74–70–73–292			
1970	71–73–71–72–287			
1971	78–71–70–74–293			
1973	70–74–72–71–287			

Alistair's aggregate of 282 in 1967 was a record at the time. The following year the altered and extended course was in use.

If the fifties belonged to Norman Thain the sixties were very definately Alistair McGregor's. One of the best Ballater born golfers, R.A. McGregor, like George Rezin, has a magnificent record on his home course and his Championship record of eleven wins is surely secure.

He was born in 1938 and admits that in his youth he spent perhaps too much time on the golf course and not enough on scholastic activities. However he became a very fine golfer and at his peak he was a master at getting down in two from 100 yards in. After schooling he spent two years in the R.A.F. and, playing for Fighter Command, reached the final of the R.A.F. Inter-Command Championship. He would have been in the team to play the final at Wentworth but was de-mobbed two weeks before the match. In December 1959 he went to work as the Cooper at the Lochnagar Distillery, Crathie, transferring to the Towiemore Distillery at Keith in 1974, from which he recently retired. Alistair married in 1965 and claims that thereafter he played his best golf.

In the Championship in 1967 no other player broke 80 and he won by 44 strokes! Last in the field of those who completed the four rounds was Fred McGregor, the brothers being first and last. But see the progress of the younger McGregor below.

In 1965 in the June medal, just prior to winning the Club Championship for the fifth time Alistair returned a 65 (a new course record because the 14th had been altered) including six consecutive threes from the eighth.

He resigned from the Ballater Club in 1978 and has since played out of Huntly, winning the championship there three times.

He won the Aboyne 36 hole Open three times. In 1965 he finished one stroke ahead of Harry Bannerman, two in front of Jack Booth, and three ahead of Ian Clark (now Turriff) and Norman Hinks. In 1970 he broke the course record (63) to finish ahead of P. Stott (Royal Aberdeen) and in 1971 he won after a count back over Ian Creswell and W.B.

Hogg. He also won at Braemar twice and at Dufftown once.

Playing in the Scott Trophy for Ballater he won the Barclay-Harvey Cup (for the best two round aggregate) four times. His afternoon 65 at Banchory in 1965 included a five and a six on the front nine!

In the final of the Aberdeen Quaich in 1969 he was beaten at the 20th by Ian Creswell. In the final of the 1965 North-east Alliance Pro-Am he and his partner, Ian Smith of Hazlehead, were beaten by Innes Wright and Ian Creswell.

As Club champion in 1971 Alistair was invited to take part in the Bon-Accord celebrations the following year. The programme notes:

> Deeside's most outstanding golfer. He has won the Ballater Championship 'many' times and holds the course record. Has won most of the events in the Dee valley several times.

Alistair gives much of the credit for his golf skill and the enjoyment the game gives him to the late Ed Stuart of Balmoral with whom he spent many hours on and off the course.

John Pringle receiving the George Rezin Memorial Shield from Rose Michie following his Club Championship win in 1968.

1984 Final of the One-Armed Golfer's Championship. John Pringle refereed the match. A.S.L. Robinson of Thorpe House beat Don Reid (Honorary Secretary of the O-A G Society) of Ravensworth G.C.

John Pringle

1968	72–71–77–78–298	2nd	I. Simpson	318
1972				
1979	75–77–75–74–301	2nd	I. Simpson	304
1983				
1984	295			
1986	80–71–77–73–301			

A very powerful and intimidating hitter, John Pringle sends the ball further down the fairway than any other member. It is said that if he could take full advantage of that he would be unbeatable.

In his early golfing years John wasn't able to play as much as some having to work in his father's garage, and also playing football. In more recent years mountaineering, and (hard) working for the Craigendarroch group has to some extent interfered with golfing opportunities.

In 1968 the third round had to be replayed because the greens became flooded by the time the leaders had played nine holes. At the end of three rounds John Pringle was leading by three strokes from R.A. McGregor who then scratched because of an injury. His brother Fred McGregor scored 331—a substantial improvement on 1967.

Barry Steel

> 1974   76–75–76–67–294, after a tie with Ian Mitchell.

Although Fred MacGregor and John Pringle were absent from this championship (they were watching the World Cup in Germany) Barry Steel beat R.E. Petrie (3), Jim Forbes (3), Ian Mitchell (4), and A.A. Mitchell (4). Steel with a final round of 67 picked up 6 shots on Ian Mitchell who was in the lead after three rounds. Steel won the 18 hole play off. The only other player to break 70 was Jim Forbes.

Barry Steel was born in Nairobi, Kenya in October 1956. He was educated at the Ballater Primary School, Aboyne Academy and St Andrews University. He learned his golf in Ballater in the junior section encouraged by local players and helped by lessons from the Murcar professional Jock Lawson who was paid by the Club to coach the juniors. At St Andrews he played occasionally for the University team. Between 1978 and 1986 he played little golf but retained his skill when, having joined the Largs Golf Club, he won the Club Championship in 1989. His present handicap is six. Ballater players say he had a beautiful swing and was a golfer of great potential.

Fred McGregor

> 1975   75–74–73–75–297
> 1977   72–74–68–75–289
> 1987   297

Fred was (and remains) a very hard working golfer. He used to practice most evenings (except Fridays of course, being the social evening!) and he became one of Ballater's best. Take 1976—he won the monthly medals in April, May, July and August scoring 73, 75, 69 and 67 respectively. He also won the Captains Prize, was runner up (to Barry Steel) in the Medal Winners Play-Off, and in the Club Championship (the year Ian Simpson broke the record with his last round 66).

Alistair McGregor, fine golfer though he was, with a house full of trophies, never achieved a scratch handicap. He acknowledges that in this respect Fred managed to go one better because in 1978 his handicap was reduced from one to scratch (for local purposes only) and he retained it for the year.

Fred was born in Ballater in 1949, Alistair's junior by eleven years (there is another brother and a sister in between), and was educated in Ballater. For a time in the seventies he worked in Aberdeen and played for the Northern Club in the League. If he is selected for the Scott Trophy again it will be for a record twentieth appearance.

There is an oft-told tale of Fred's brush with a policeman in the car park in Banchory. He had been playing golf in Elgin, had consumed the good golfer's ration in the bar and had been driven back to Banchory to

91

Barry Steel (top) the Largs Golf Champion in 1989 and (below) the Ballater Champion in 1974 with Ian Simpson who had won the Mary Hynd trophy.

await a promised lift to Ballater. Tired from his golfing exertions he lay down on a bench with his clubs beside him. 'Far are ye goin?', 'Ballater' says Fred. The conversation proceeded gingerly while the policemen sized up the situation. Finally, staring at the golf clubs, he asked 'Far did ye come fey?', 'Wimbledon', says Fred. End of polite conversation!

There is another story which may conveniently be told at this point although it has nothing whatever to do with Fred. Fishermen's tales and golfer's stories have this in common—they both have a degree of exaggeration and, sometimes, improbability. They say, in the bar at the Ballater Golf Club, that a couple of the best golfers in the Club used to go out on the course of an evening carrying an almost empty golf bag. Having played a few holes they would hook a drive, bringing them close to the Minister's 'Pot', from whence they would pull a fish. Resuming the round they would eventually reach the Clubhouse with a ten pounder neatly enclosed in the bag. The exaggeration, of course, is that it was only a six pounder—the improbability remains!

I. Simpson

1976	79–79–74–66–298	2nd	F. McGregor	304
1990	75–73–76–74–298	2nd	J.F. Hardie	298

A Ballater man, born in 1943, and educated locally. After leaving school Ian joined Gordon Fraser, the former Building Contractor but left to join the Lochnagar Distillery in 1972 where he worked his way up until he was appointed Brewer in 1987.

Ian took up golf in the early sixties working his handicap down from 21 in 1963 to around 10 by the end of the decade. In the seventies he made steady progress getting down to 3 in 1977. He has remained in the lower single figure area ever since. His record in the Championship, although including only two wins, is impressive. He has been second on at least four occasions (probably more but the records are incomplete), and third, fourth, or fifth several times.

In 1990 Simpson and Hardie were tied after four rounds requiring a play-off (the first for 16 years) over 18 holes. Simpson won with 75 beating Hardie by one shot. They were tied on the 18th tee but Hardie's drive was bunkered and he failed to match Ian's par. His 66 in 1976 was a record, beating the 67 by Fred McGregor a few days earlier.

J.F. Hardie

1978	71–80–66–76–293			
1982	75–74–73–74–296			
1985	69–73–71–75–288			
1988	76–80–75–74–305			
1989	73–74–75–74–296			
1991	69–71–72–68–280	2nd	F. McGregor	290

93

Jim Hardie was born in Ballater in November 1941. Jim has achieved many fine results, for example on 8th April 1990 playing in the McLean Cup in most difficult Ballater conditions he scored a gross 67 (net 66) with the following figures 534434533—34, and 444334524—33. This, on a day when the CSS was 71 and no other player broke 80! He and Fraser Mann won the Alliance Cup in 1990 at Murcar—apart from a missed putt of ten feet or so at the first and an overstrong approach at the second Jim made no mistakes.

He played golf from the earliest possible age and when the family moved to Aberdeen around 1950 he joined Bon-Accord. He moved to New Zealand in 1966 with a handicap of 8—on his return in 1973 he had reduced it to one. In 1975 he joined Hazlehead where he won the Club Championship (beating A.K. Pirie in the semi-final).

In 1991 in his fiftieth year Hardie recorded the lowest aggregate since the competition started in 1953 and it was the first time any winner has scored two rounds under 70.

Jim Hardie has never won the Ballater Open but he continues to play fine golf off a handicap of one and he may yet accomplish the feat. In 1989, following recovery from a major operation, he was selected to play for the North-east District against the North District at Inverness. Commenting on this selection, Colin Farquharson in the *Press and Journal*:

> Hardie has come back in his forties, from a major operation to play some of the finest golf of his life. The gritty player . . . can have an abrasive exterior at times . . . [but] Hardie has earned a place in the side.

J. Forbes

1980	74–75–74–74–297			
1981	75–78–72–72–297	2nd	I. Simpson	301

Jim Forbes was born in Aboyne in 1941. The Forbes' are a very well known Deeside golfing family. The mixed foursomes partnership of Helen (his wife) and Jim has won many trophies. Helen took up golf following the birth of their fourth child and now plays off four! Jim's brother Donald has won the Aboyne Championship 17 times to Jim's four but Donald has never had a handicap lower than Jim. Both work for Grampian Regional Council.

Garry, the oldest son is assistant professional at Deeside. Steven is 'offshore' and plays to one. Julie is a professional on the British Tour and finally Colin is an assistant greenkeeper at Aboyne and plays off two.

In 1980 Jim won by four shots from Fred McGregor and John Pringle who were tied at 301.

*   *   *

During the forty or so years since the Club Championship started it has been dominated by Alistair McGregor, John Pringle, and Jim Hardie. Had Ian Clark not left the district he would no doubt have captured more titles. These golfers plus the others who occasionally won the title can be regarded (at any rate in the locality) as very good golfers. Some of them can be so described in terms of north-east golf.

There are others who have been very nearly, very good golfers. None has won the championship—some have come very close, none closer than Ian Mitchell (with the John Daly swing) when he tied in 1974 but lost the play-off to Barry Steel. Another very fine golfer who showed great promise when he was playing at Ballater was Bruce Illingworth. His problem was Alistair McGregor!

TEN

The Ballater Open

At a meeting on 7th May 1931, J. Keiller Greig, supported by George Rezin, proposed that the Club hold an open tournament. It was decided to raise it at a Special meeting (called to discuss Sunday play) on 10th June. The idea was approved. A thirty six hole tournament would be held on Saturday 15th August. Thirteen members guaranteed £1 each towards the expenses.

1931. There were 45 entries. The winner was 'local champion' G.M. Rezin (5) with 154. George holing a long putt across the last green. Second and third were G.N. Gordon, Deeside (3), 155, and A. Fraser, Bon-Accord, 156.

Other competitors included D.R. MacDonald, Royal Aberdeen (1) who led after the first round with A. Fraser, both on 76, J.G. Elmslie, Royal Aberdeen (3), C. Symon, Victoria, (4), J.W.L. Bain, Aberdeen University, (5), A.W. Porter, Murcar, (6), J. Fraser, Braemar, (2), Dr W.B. Brodie Brown, Aboyne, (4), J. Grosert, Deeside, (3), and W. Lumsden, Caledonian, (3).

Local players included, Rev. J. Grant, Colonel A.E. Stewart, I.J. Findlay, and H. Knowles.

Peter Craighead commented in the *Press and Journal*:

BALLATER'S FIRST TOURNEY

The list of open amateur golf tournaments in the north of Scotland grows longer. Ballater is the latest name to be added, and the town had its first taste of an open tournament on Saturday last.

The taste was to Ballater's liking, leaving behind it an appetite for more open tournaments.

I turned my back on the Coiles of Muick on Saturday night with the feeling that from small beginnings great things are to accrue.

In following the lead of Banchory by promoting a one-day tournament Ballater is offering increased opportunities in competitive golf to many golfers unable to participate in three-day tournaments. For that alone Ballater's enterprise is to be commended.

One of the features of the first Ballater tournament was the high scoring — not the result of unfavourable weather conditions or the absence of golfing talent. The high scores . . . showed what the people of Ballater have known for a long time. They have . . . a course worthy of the greatest respect.

I confess to being one of those who . . . thought the Ballater course, with its smooth fairways, [was] waiting quietly to yield fantastically low scores. The narrow fairways and Dr Mackenzie [the famous golf course architect] with his closely-bunkered greens, quickly disillusioned me.

The following note appeared in another north-east newspaper:

The first open tournament staged by the Ballater Club proved quite a success, and it is perhaps appropriate that the young local champion, G.M. Rezin should prove the winner.

An entry of 45 was not nearly as good as it might have been, and it is . . . disappointing that it did not have wider appeal.

The tournament ran very smoothly under the guidance of the enthusiastic officials, and perhaps by next year their patience and enthusiasm will reap its just reward.

Finally — the tournament accounts showed a loss of £16–8–6 — the Club decided to carry this and the guarantors were not called upon.

1932. A good field of 48 players including some of the best in the North-East — H.R. Dey, Deeside (Scratch), J. Fraser, Braemar (2), W. Watt, Stonehaven (1), Dr J.G. Elmslie, Royal Aberdeen (3), A. Fraser, Bon-Accord (3), J.R.S. Cruickshank, Royal Aberdeen (4), J.A.S. Glennie, Peterhead (Scr), G.N. Gordon, Royal Aberdeen (2), J.W.L. Bain, Aberdeen University (3), W.A. Richmond, Montrose (2), and of course G.M. Rezin (3).

At lunch Rezin, 75, was in the lead 4 ahead of W.A. Richmond and J. Fraser, with J.A.S. Glennie a further shot behind. In the afternoon Rezin faltered with a 77 for 152, and Glennie beat him by one stroke with 71, a course record, for 151.

The *Press and Journal* reporter commenting on the weather wrote:

Saturday's competitors had to contend with a wind which at times blew with gale force, only four of the competitors succeeding in breaking 80.

1933. Over 80 competitors played in oppressive heat. Of the 13 Ballater entrants only George Rezin (75 and 76) and H. Knowles (77 and 75) broke 80 in both rounds. Rezin finished fifth behind R.S. Walker, the winner, W.A. Richmond, A.R. Grosert (Murcar), and G.N. Gordon.

R.S. Walker, Aberdeen University (2), in his first appearance in the event, and second in the morning with 74, equalled the course record of 71 (145) in the afternoon to win by 4 strokes from W.A. Richmond, Montrose (149). Walker had recently won the prestigious Moray Open at Lossiemouth, the runner-up being Donald Cameron (Kirkintilloch) (see Appendix Three).

In the 1930's all Ballater competitions were decided on net scores. The Committee for the Open had laid down a 'Second Round Qualifying' rule which, in this competition, produced an absurd situation, as Peter Craighead reported:

> With entries close on and beyond the 100 mark, the promoters of the Banchory and Ballater tournaments have been faced with the problem of having to squeeze two rounds of play into the one day.
>
> A process of reducing the number of competitors at the end of the first round has been evolved.... At Ballater the condition is, 'Those whose net scores fall within ten strokes of the lowest net score returned in the first round will qualify for the second round'. This can, at times, deal harshly with the scratch and low handicap golfers.
>
> At Ballater a big handicap golfer, hitting the high spots during an inspired hour, would have robbed the tourney at the half-way stage of some of its prominent personalities had not a hurried meeting of the tournament committee been called to consider the situation. The result of the meeting was that the qualifying net score should be 80 and under.
>
> The man who created the stir was D.G. Dempster (Murcar) a nine handicap golfer who returned a card of 73 in the first round giving a net score of 64. Thus the qualifying [cut] would have fallen at a net score of 74, eliminating the two scratch men ... J.A.S. Glennie, Peterhead, winner last year, W. Watt, Stonehaven, and other good golfers.
>
> Just how unjust a qualifying test based on net scores in a tournament in which the championship goes to the leading scratch aggregate might be to scratch and low handicap golfers may be gleaned from the fact that last year Glennie qualified ... with a first round of 80, and went on to win the title by breaking the course record in the second round.

Dempster won the handicap prize with a net 137.

1934. Former winners, G.M. Rezin, (Scratch), J.A.S. Glennie, (2) and R.S. Walker competed. New entrants included Logie Bain, and Lewis Middleton, of Aberdeen University, and W.N. Stewart, Royal Aberdeen. Twenty years later Middleton won a newspaper award naming him as the leading amateur golfer in the north-east.

The winner was W.A. Richmond (Montrose) with a record breaking round of 69 followed by 71. Richmond had been runner up the previous year and 3rd in 1932. The next five were W.N. Stewart 145, Lewis Middleton 146, J.A.S. Glennie 149, R.S. Walker 150, and George Rezin 151.

The last two players went out at 4 p.m. and finished at 6.15!

1935. 'Sun-baked fairways, and greens full of tricks'—thus Peter Craighead explained the high all round scoring. The field of 85 was led by the well known West of Scotland golfer Don Cameron, (Kirkintilloch) who scored two 73's to win by three shots from George Rezin and R.S. Walker who both finished with 149. Walker had just won the Moray Open for the second time, defeating Don Cameron again. W. Richmond, last year's winner was fourth. He was followed by a bevy of University golfers including J.W.L. Bain and J.M. Geddie.

Other 73's were scored by R.S. Walker, G.M. Rezin, and G.K. Ironside (8) of Ballater. G.K. Ironside followed his first round of 84 with 73 and finished third in the Handicap, the winner being Alan Gibb (16).

1936. A newspaper note prior to the 1936 open reads:

Ballater's open amateur tournament will be on August 1st. The course is in grand trim. Even during the drought it was a delight to play on.

Among those who will be in the hunt for the handsome prizes—there are none better at any of the one-day tournaments around us—will be no fewer than nine from the Aberdeen Football Club.

The weather, particularly after lunch was awful and Peter Craighead said this about a day which saw the end of the drought:

Rezin won the title ... he had a second round of 73, [following 75] a gallant effort during which for four holes he was blinded and drenched by a deluge. The afternoon was marred by heavy rain, but there were earlier spells of bright sunshine, during which this charming Deeside course was a pleasant place on which to play and watch golf.

But the pleasure of those sunshiny minutes was forgotten when many of the players and onlookers, who had set out without waterproofs and umbrellas were drenched. . . .

The day had ended in a tie between Rezin and J.S. Murray, (Stonehaven) a member of the Aberdeen City Police force, Rezin being awarded the title for the better second round.

A special prize was awarded to J. Howie, Ballater's war-disabled one-armed golfer who completed both rounds.

1937. The headlines read:

G. REZIN'S THIRD SUCCESS

George M. Rezin, the well-known Ballater player, retained the Ballater open amateur title when the sixth annual tournament was played over the Ballater course on Saturday. Rezin tied with W. Watt, Stonehaven but had the better second round.

It was a grand day for golf, the only unsettling factor being a fairly strong wind which rose when the first round was about half completed. The sun shone brilliantly, while the course was in excellent condition—the best it has ever been this time of the year.

99

Once again the scoring was relatively high but the field was perhaps of a lower quality than in any of the previous years. Rezin scored two 75's, W. Watt a 73 and 77, and behind them came J.S. Murray (last year's runner-up) 79 and 73, and H.R. Dey (Deeside) two 76's.

A.G. Gibb was the best local (after Rezin) with 79 and 81.

1938. George Rezin again! His third win in a row and his fourth in the eight years since the tournament started. Now wearing a Deeside Golf Club shirt (his career had taken him into Aberdeen) George left no room for doubt about the win this time; he scored 143, beating A.S. Finnie of Aberdeen University by five shots.

J. Fraser of Braemar was third having tied with Rezin for the first round lead with 72.

Three other University golfers finished in the first seven — D.G. Dempster, R. Semple, and G.S. Riddell. W. Elmslie, the Banchory Town Clerk, had the distinction of doing the inward half in 34 (best of the day) during his second round of 77.

1939. The newspaper reported:

> Golf in the heatwave ... the sun blazed down from a cloudless sky and there was little or no wind. The only problem was the varying pace of the greens as they dried quickly in the hot sunshine after overnight frost.

Quentin Murray of Royal Aberdeen won with 146, playing the course for the first time. George Rezin tied for second place, 4 strokes behind, along with three others — J. Fraser, Braemar, J.J.M. Thomson, Murcar, and G.M. Bisset, Edinburgh University.

Ballater golfer G.K. Ironside (5) hit the headlines by leading the field with a 73 in the morning but he finished sixth.

*   *   *

Let's pause for a moment; the thirties are all but over, war is less than a month ahead, and the next Ballater tournament will be played in 1946. The first nine years of the open belong to George Rezin — four wins, second three times, a fifth, and a sixth! He will play in a few more opens but the thirties were his great years.

*   *   *

1946. Conditions were ideal. The course looked good in blazing sunshine although early starters (from 9 a.m. at five minute intervals) found it a 'trifle stiff' after some overnight and early morning rain.

The afternoon paper on 3rd August reports:

> Nearly half the field were from the Deeside, Royal Aberdeen, and Murcar clubs.
>
> Entries included G.M. Rezin (Scratch), Hugh Willox (2) Deeside, a finalist in the Aberdeen Quaich yesterday, and Quentin Murray (5) Royal

Aberdeen, the 1939 winner.

Other well known players competing included Lewis Middleton, Royal Aberdeen, H.R. Dey, and H.G. Stephen, Deeside, and J.W. Booth, from Murcar.

In the morning W.N. Stewart, Royal Aberdeen, led with 74 but at the end of play A. Mathieson, Banchory, had won with 75 and 73 (best round of the day) for 148. Second was Hector Dey of Deeside (151), and third W.R.S. Mellis of Royal Aberdeen (152).

Best Ballater performances were by George Leith (82, 78), and I. Findlay (79, 81) equal 13th. Dr M. Gibb won the handicap.

1947. Hugh Willox, Deeside, was the winner with 145, two shots clear of J.G. M'Gregor, Hazlehead, (147), and four shots ahead of George Rezin, (149), who recovered some of the form he lost in 1946. J.W. Booth (Murcar) finished equal 7th with 75 and 80. Norman Thain was well up the field with two rounds under 80.

The Handicap winner was A.H. Bain, Murcar.

1948. The Monday newspaper reported:

Sandy Black, the young Aberdeen University golfer, recorded his second tournament success in a month when he followed up his Braemar success by taking first place at Ballater with rounds of 72 and 71 for 143 to beat George Rezin, by two strokes.

It was a meritorious performance by the student, who finished third in the Boyd Quaich at St Andrews on Friday and did not reach his home until midnight.

Black, partnered by Tommy Pearson [Aberdeen F.C.] soon showed evidence of his ... hitting powers and far outdrove his partner.

Norman Thain remembers a Black drive from the second tee which 'carried' the Ladies tee at the first!

At the 18th in the morning Rezin holed his pitch for a two.

1949. Sandy Black (with two others from the Cambridge University team) returned to defend his title but 74 and 75 left him trailing by three shots from the winner Hector Dey (Deeside), who won with the better afternoon round, from Dr J.M. Geddie (Royal Aberdeen), both scoring 146.

George Rezin was third with two 74's and, to nobody's surprise, he holed his pitch to the eighteenth in the morning.

The handicap winner was G.K. Knowles (9) 137.

1950. Newspaper comment included the following:

Ballater Golf Club's one-day open amateur tournament must surely be one of the best organised. The officials there always get things running smoothly.

It is no easy job to get a field of more than 100 players twice round in one day, but Mr John Worling, the starter, had everyone off the tee early for the second round.

Inside the clubhouse the women members did grand service with teas for competitors and friends. Very warm thanks are due to Mr Rezin and his committee for a grand day's work.

The first winner of the Lochnagar Shield (donated as a perpetual prize by Captain Frai) was A.L. Downs of Royal Aberdeen with rounds of 70 and 71 for 141. On 142 (two 71's) came footballer Tommy Pearson a stroke ahead of George Rezin who tied for third place with A.C. Farquharson (Royal Aberdeen).

Another well known Aberdeen footballer, Matt Armstrong, had an excellent 73 in the morning but fell away after lunch.

Good Ballater performances were recorded by I.J. Findlay (148), N. Thain (149), and Dr A.G. Gibb (149).

1951. A.A. Middleton of Cruden Bay won the Lochnagar Shield with 69, 71 for 140. Tied second, on 143, were Tommy Pearson (Murcar) and H.G. Stephen (Deeside).

At the Club A.G.M. in March, George Rezin (Captain) was elected an honorary life member in recognition of his services to the club. In this, his penultimate open appearance, he recorded a poor performance, by his standards. Two 78's left him far down the field. This must have been one of 'those' days since his recent scores in Club competitions, reflected his true class.

Ballater players finishing ahead of Rezin, included Norman Thain and I.J. Findlay (both 153) and Dr A.G. Gibb (154). The Handicap was won by R. Barron (Aboyne), with Vic Shepherd second.

1952. Quentin Murray's year and George Rezin's last. In his first round Murray equalled Rezin's record of 67 and a second round of 74 making 141 was enough to win the open for the second time. J.K. Hall (Royal Aberdeen), Tommy Pearson, and Grant Spaeth (U.S.A.) were equal second. George Rezin (144) was fifth.

Norman McLeod remembers playing on his own one evening, hitting (for him at the time) a splendid shot to the (then) thirteenth green with his driver and then being approached by a young man who asked if he might join in. Invited to do so Grant Spaeth (for it was he) took out a four iron and hit a beauty through the green. Spaeth was visiting relatives in Ballater. He was from Stanford University, California and was in Scotland to play in the students' international Boyd Quaich at St Andrews. The newspaper report of this event described him as 'the long hitting . . .'. In 1991 Grant Spaeth completed his two-year term as President of the U.S. Golf Association — one of the most prestigious titles in the golfing world. He works in Palo Alto, California. In a recent letter he writes:

I will be back to Ballater sometime soon. I am a member of the Royal and

Ancient and never pass up a visit to Ballater when I am there, usually during the Autumn Medal. . . . Have a great centenary year. I love that golf course.

1953. In the morning Wallace Anderson, Stonehaven, played brilliantly scoring 34 out and 35 back. Anderson's partner, Dr J.M. Geddie (Royal Aberdeen) returned a 68 in the afternoon to win the prize for the best round of the day. Geddie's was a fine round, mostly played in the heavy rain which pushed scores up.

At the end of the day Wallace Anderson won with an aggregate of 144, one shot more than A. Cordiner (Murcar). Harry Stephen was third on 146 and the holder, Quentin Murray, was fourth a further stroke behind. The leading Ballater player was I.D.R. Clark (149).

1954. The 'green' *Evening Express* had this to say:

MIRACLE 63 AT BALLATER

Stewart Murray, a young Renfrewshire golfer, who has been a member of the West District team this year, returned a sensational 63 in the first round of the Ballater Golf Club's one-day tournament today.

This beat the previous record by four strokes. Murray, who travelled overnight from Glasgow had never seen the course before and started off badly by incurring a penalty stroke on the first hole where he used his brassie from the tee and put his ball in the ditch.

For the first eight holes he was level 4's with no hint of the sensational scoring to follow. He drove the ninth green using his spoon, and holed a two-yard putt for a two and an outward half of 34. On the inward journey his approach play was so accurate that he required only 11 putts in the nine holes. On the last green he had a putt from two yards for a 62 but the ball ran right round the rim of the cup and failed to drop. In all he had 25 putts.

At the end of the afternoon, however, the result was a win for Innes Wright (138) by virtue of his better second round: Innes Wright (Aboyne) 70, 68; S.T.W. Murray (Elderslie) 63, 75. Jack Booth was third on 139, followed by J.P. Grant (Deeside).

Norman Thain who in 1953 had won the first Ballater Club Championship finished 6th with rounds of 69 and 73—the best ever performance by a local player (apart from the late George Rezin). Dr Gibb and I.D.R. Clark finished equal on 152.

1955. The recent winners at Aboyne and Braemar, Eric Buthley (Royal Aberdeen), and Tommy Pearson (Murcar) were in the field. The winning aggregate of 147 was the highest since the War and was attributed to the very fast greens.

Ian Hardie, (a product of the Banff school of golfers which includes Jack Booth, and J.J.M. Thomson), but now playing out of Hazlehead

103

won with 74, 73, two shots better than Norman Hinks (Banchory) who opened with 77 but then had the best round of the day — 72. Eddie Main of Murcar was equal second and Innes Wright (last year's winner) was fourth after a tie with John Grant and Hector Dey, both of Deeside. A prodigious hitter Hardie one day scored an eagle at the first at Hazlehead, driving the green and sinking the putt.

W.M. (Bill) Crighton was in good company on 160 with Ian Phillips (Ballater) and Eric Buthlay (Royal Aberdeen). Crighton went on (21 years later) to win the U.K. Seniors title at The Berkshire.

1956. The first open to be played in three's. 7.15 a.m. start.

Jack Booth (Scratch) of Murcar won the trophy with a record aggregate of 135. A round of 68 in the morning tied with Wallace Anderson (Falkirk) but 67 in the afternoon left Booth the winner by three strokes. Booth's round of 67 included a 7 at the third and 31 for the back nine. George Smith led the local players.

1957. Norman Hinks (Banchory) won with a total of 141 (72 and 69). The holder Jack Booth was second on 143 and consistent Tommy Pearson was third on 148. Norman McLeod was the best local player (153). Dr A.G. Gibb (8) won the Handicap.

1958. 'Round the clock golf' they called it in the press. The first pair teed off at 7.30 a.m. and at the end of the day the last pair started at 5.10 p.m!

John Grant (Deeside) with 71, 70 won by two shots from Ian Clark, 72, 71. Innes Wright was third.

1959. Innes Wright broke the record with an aggregate of 131 (67 and 64). In a magnificent days golf he had one 2, and one 5 (at the 1st in the morning) — otherwise it was a collection of 3's and 4's. Norman Hinks was second (136) and J.J.M. Thomson of Murcar third (141). Norman Thain and George Smith tied on 152.

1960. Because of a violent storm, the afternoon round was played over the first nine holes only. Newton Henderson, 68, 34, and Jack Booth, 67, 35, both of Murcar tied for first place the win going to Henderson with his better afternoon score.

1961. In the morning. Newton Henderson (Murcar) and Innes Wright tied for the lead with 68's. The leading Ballater golfer, three strokes behind, was Bruce Illingworth. Other well known players in handy positions were Hector Dey (70), J.W. Booth (72), and J. Forbes (73).

After lunch Henderson returned 70 for 138 two ahead of Illingworth. Jack Booth and W.G. Scott (Murcar) were equal third.

R.A. McGregor, Club Champion, (146), finished equal 10th, winning the local scratch. Angus Davidson was equal first in the handicap while his brother, Roger Davidson won the James Ferrier trophy for the best handicap round, (9) 65.

1962. Entries 110. Monday newspaper comment:

TOM FROST STILL IN TOP FORM

Tom Frost, the Montrose golfer, claimed his second tournament success in two days with the narrowest of victories in the Ballater open one day golf tournament on Saturday.

Frost, who won at Montrose on Friday, gained the decision over Ian Clark, (Turriff) on the strength of his last six holes in the second round.

Both Clark and Frost returned 68 in the morning to establish a five-stroke lead over the rest of the field. They failed to maintain their form in the second round each scoring 40 out and 36 back for 76's.

Last year's winner, Newton Henderson, and George Rutherford also of Murcar, tied with aggregates of 146, two behind the leaders.

Ian Clark was the best of the Ballater players. Norman McLeod had opened with a 75 but lost form in the afternoon.

A gale force wind blew in the morning and although conditions improved later there were showers and the scoring was high.

J.A.S. Glennie (Cruden Bay) returning to the scene of his triumph in 1932 scored 75 and 76 to be equal 9th on 151.

1963. A three way tie on 142 between Ian Phillips, his brother Ivor Phillips, and Sandy Pirie. The Championship went to Ian, who had the better 2nd round, from Ivor, who finished ahead of Pirie by virtue of the better finishing holes. Ian Phillips was getting his own back on Sandy Pirie who had won after a tie at Braemar a few weeks earlier.

Other 69's were recorded by Norman Hinks (Banchory) and James Forbes (Aboyne). Ballater member Norman McLeod was 4th.

1964. Sandy Pirie, in top form, put together two rounds of 72, for his sixth win, finishing two ahead of I.D.R. Clark. Bruce Illingworth and M.S. Robertson (Aboyne) were equal third.

The best rounds were 70's by R.A. McGregor and Ian Phillips.

1965. Sandy Pirie (139) returned to win again. A 71 and then 68 left him three shots clear of Ian Clark who was again second. D. Forbes (Aboyne) was third and Alistair McGregor, fourth.

A new name appears—J. Pringle (9) scored 78 and 76 to win the second handicap prize. The winner was Gordon Christie (9) from Broomieknowe, Edinburgh.

1966. Sandy Pirie wins for the third successive year. He followed a morning 72 with a fine 65 to win by three shots from Ivor Phillips who had scored 69 and 71. Alistair McGregor was third on 142, Ian Creswell fourth, and Ian Clark fifth with 147.

Steve Eggo (14), the one-armed golfer from St Andrews won the Handicap.

A couple of weeks later Pirie went to Banchory where he won the

Open with rounds of 63 (including a lost ball penalty) and 66 finishing seven shots ahead of the field. Then, in early September he broke the course record at Ballater, going round in 64 to win the 18 hole Open by three shots from Ian Clark.

1967. Ian Creswell, Hazlehead Champion, and winner of the Simmers Trophy, (Aberdeen links championship), won with rounds of 70 and 71. R. Brechin (Northern) was second with a couple of 72's, and I.D.R. Clark was third with 71 and 74.

1968. Ballater's I.D.R. Clark (142) won the Open for the first time having been runner up three times. The Press reported that Ian had now won every trophy on the Deeside circuit.

R.L. Nicol (Murcar) was second on 143. John Chillas (Royal Aberdeen) was equal third with D. Forbes (Aboyne).

Local players featuring in the handicap were J.G. Smith (8) who was third and A. Grant (9) equal fifth.

1969. Eric Morrison (Hazlehead) won with 139. Second equal were A.G. Booth (Murcar), R. Brechin (Northern), and A.K. Pirie.

Alistair McGregor was a disappointing fifth after a first round of 66. John Pringle finished on 151.

Handicap prizes were won by Leslie Sandison (16) who was first and E. Murray second.

1970.

R.A. McGregor	Ballater	141
B. Dignan	Hazlehead	143
N. Hinks	Banchory	145

1967 Rev R.H.G. Budge of Crathie with Mrs Budge presents the Lochnagar Shield to Ian Creswell. Harry Wright the club captain and Anne (right) look on.

The Handicap was won by R. Petrie (11) 63 and 65 net.

A.K. Pirie was engaged elsewhere — he was playing (and winning) for Great Britain in Belgium.

1971. No distractions this year for Sandy Pirie who won convincingly by five strokes from Alistair McGregor, with Ian Creswell a further stroke behind.

The scores were:

A.K. Pirie	68–66	134
R.A. McGregor	72–67	139
I.F. Creswell	72–70	142

The leading handicap winners were all Ballater golfers: Jim Clark (11) 138 was first. John Pringle (3), Sandy Grant (5), and Fred McGregor (3) were second equal.

1972. The lunchtime leader was J. Tait (Caledonian) two ahead of John Pringle and R.L. Nicol (Banchory). H.D.S. Adam (Hazlehead) and R.A. McGregor were on 73 and they tied for first place with 71's in the afternoon. McGregor won on the count back.

Equal third were D. Hird (Murcar), and J.H. Little (Royal Aberdeen) on 145 while Ian Creswell was fifth with 146.

1973. Ian Creswell (Hazlehead) won by two shots from Gordon Nicol (Deeside). The scores were:

Ian Creswell	68–71	139
Gordon Nicol	72–69	141
Sandy Pirie	73–69	142

Ballater was well represented among the Handicap winners:

R.C. Moir	(7)	136
I. Rankine	(7)	137
R. Hardman	(8)	141
F. Anderson	(8)	141

1974. There were 99 entries. Sandy Pirie won (for the fifth time) from local member D.J. Walker with the better afternoon round. The scores were:

A.K. Pirie	(Hazlehead)	69–74	143
D.J. Walker	(Ballater)	68–75	143
R.A. McGregor	(Ballater)	71–73	144

Derek J. Walker, of the Clydesdale Bank (currently managing Duff-town and Rothes) was a member of the Ballater and Aboyne Clubs for a couple of years when he worked in Aboyne. In a letter he recalls the ordeal of the afternoon round when for the first time in his life he had to play in front of a crowd of spectators. A long time single figure golfer he has also been a member of Hazlehead, Royal Aberdeen, Fort Wil-

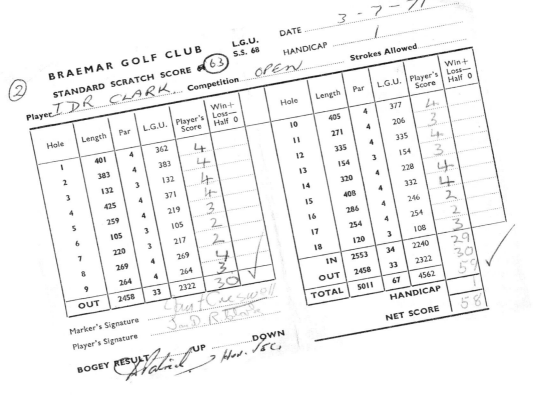

BRAEMAR GOLF CLUB L.G.U. S.S. 68

DATE 3-7-71

HANDICAP 1

STANDARD SCRATCH SCORE 63

Strokes Allowed

Player I D R CLARK Competition OPEN

Hole	Length	Par	L.G.U.	Player's Score	Win+ Loss— Half 0
1	401	4	362	4	
2	383	4	383	4	
3	132	3	132	4	
4	425	4	371	4	
5	259	4	219	3	
6	105	3	105	2	
7	220	3	217	2	
8	269	4	269	4	
9	264	4	264	3	
OUT	2458	33	2322	30	✓

Hole	Length	Par	L.G.U.	Player's Score	Win+ Loss— Half 0
10	405	4	377	4	
11	271	4	206	3	
12	335	4	335	4	
13	154	3	154	3	
14	320	4	228	4	
15	408	4	332	4	
16	286	4	246	2	
17	254	4	254	2	
18	120	3	108	3	
IN	2553	34	2240	29	
OUT	2458	33	2322	30	
TOTAL	5011	67	4562	59	✓

HANDICAP 1

NET SCORE 58

Marker's Signature _Iant Creswell_

Player's Signature _Jan D R Blane_

BOGEY RESULT _Alalid_ UP _Hon. ISC_ DOWN

Young Ian Clark showing his long follow-through.

Harry Wright says congratulations.

108

ABOVE *The 1972 Ballater Open. Alistair McGregor receives the trophy from Vice-Captain Bob Law.*

BELOW *Sandy Pirie, wearing his Walker Cup jacket, receives the Ballater Open trophy from Ballater's last Provost, Miss Briscoe.*

109

liam, Fort Augusta, Lossiemouth, and Dufftown where he was Captain in 1988 when the course was extended to eighteen holes. He was a member of the Bankers team which won the Aberdeen Trades four-somes in 1979.

The Handicap scores included:

Jim Clark	(7)	135	2nd
E. Murray	(15)	138	4th

1975. Ian Creswell a recent quarter-finalist in the Scottish Amateur continued his good form with a three shot win.

Ian Creswell	(R. Aberdeen)	71–74	145
Sandy Watson	(Deeside)	73–75	148
Derek Brown	(Northern)	75–74	149

In the handicap I.G.K. Phillips (Aberdeen Nomads) was third on 142, first prize having been won by C.A. Nicol (Dufftown).

1976.

Sandy Pirie	(Hazlehead)	72–66	138
Dennis Christie	(Banchory)	68–71	139
Jimmy Wood	(Caledonian)	73–68	141

In the second round Sandy Pirie equalled the record for the course which had been altered in 1967. Ian Simpson had established the record 66 when he won the Club Championship a few weeks earlier.

The Handicap prize went to J. Sangster (Little Aston) whose net 130 beat H. Henderson's 133 (Buchanan Castle).

1977.

David Hird	(Murcar)	75–67	142
John Johnston	(Royal Aberdeen)	69–75	144
Ronnie Brechin	(Northern)	77–68	145

The local Scratch prize was won By Fred McGregor—148.

The Handicap Prize went to Angus Davidson (6) 136. Second was D.J. Walker (Royal Aberdeen) (5) 137.

1978. This was the first occasion when the *Press and Journal* carried no report about the Open—just the leading Scratch and Handicap scores:

G.S. Wood	(Deeside)	139
F.J. Coutts	,,	140
J.F. Hardie	(Hazlehead)	142

Frank Coutts turned professional in 1984 and has remained at the Deeside Club.

Handicap prizes went to: Barry Steel (6) and Angus Davidson (6) who each finished on 140, Steel winning on the count back.

110

1979.

A.J. Eddie	(Hazlehead)	138
J.F. Hardie	(Ballater)	142
J. Forbes	(Aboyne)	143

Jim Hardie, third last year, improves to second place and his after-noon round of 68 wins the best scratch prize.

Three Ballater members headed the handicap:

I.D.R. Clark	(7)	138
A.W.B. Davidson	(4)	139
R.G.B. Davidson	(4)	139

1980.

The 1980 Open was won by David Hird (Murcar) who scored two 72's for 144. D. Jamieson (Nigg Bay) was second—145 and E. Lindsay (Caledonian) was third with 145 also. Barry Steel won the Handicap.

1981. Donald Jamieson of Nigg Bay was the winner with 71 and 67, the best round of the day. 'The young Murcar player' Keith Hird (David's son) was second, 69 and 71. Local members Angus Davidson (77–71) and Barry Steel (69–79) were equal sixth.

Ballater members were well to the fore in the handicap prizes, Bill Roy (11) was first, Roger Davidson, second and M. Mather and E.R. Hardman equal third.

1982.

John Pringle	(Ballater)	141
John Cramond	(Hazlehead)	143
Raymond Cheyne	(Nigg Bay)	143

Pringle, who had been Club Champion in 1969, 1972, and 1979, won the Open for the first time—the first Ballater member to win since Alistair McGregor in 1972.

Handicap prizes went to:

H. Henderson	(Buchanan Castle)	(18)	135
S. Price	(Murcar)	(4)	135
S. Bain	(Inverurie)	(11)	135

1983. The Sports pages of the Monday paper on this morning were crowded with Golf results from all over the North-east. On the same day as the Ballater Open there were 'Opens' at Banchory, Boat of Garten, Forres, Huntly, Moray, Peterhead, Torphins, and Westhill. In addition medal results, which had been played on either Saturday or Sunday at twenty clubs, were reported. The effect of this, of course, is that the best north-east players are distributed throughout the area in these competitions rather than being seen on one of a very few courses—as was the case in days gone by. Be that as it may there were many more fine

111

golfers around although they may not have been such well known 'names'. As usual there was some fine golf in the Ballater Open:

J. Cramond	(Hazlehead)	71–68	139
G. Wood	(Nigg Bay)	68–72	140
J.G. Wood	(Westhill)	74–69	143
F.H. McGregor	(Ballater)	73–70	143
J. Pringle	„	72–71	143

A few weeks later playing in the one-round Ballater Open, John Cramond (2) broke the course record with a 64.

The Handicap event produced a Ballater winner:

D. McKendrick	(Ballater)	(12)	126
F. Wright	(Nigg Bay)	(8)	127
R.C. Burnett	(Murcar)	(14)	130

1984.

G. Gordon	(Nigg Bay)	141
R.A. Cheyne	(Northern)	142
A. Howie	„	143

Handicap

P. Simon	(Batchwood, St Albans)	(18)	123
W. Rose	(Panmure)	(11)	129
A. McRae	(Ballater)	(10)	133

The best local scratch score was 145 by John Pringle. Roger Davidson (9) won the Handicap with 136.

1985.

A. Cruickshank	(Caledonian)	146
J.F. Hardie	(Ballater/Hazlehead)	147
R.A. Cheyne	(Northern)	147

Handicap

A. Duguid	(Ballater)	(17)	131
S. Brown	(Ruxley, Kent)	(13)	135
M. Hosie	(Murcar)	(7)	135

The best local scratch was 149 by F.H. McGregor and E. Smith (12) won the local Handicap with 137.

1986.

A. Cruickshank	(Caledonian)	139
K. Hird	(Murcar)	147
R.G. Petrie	(Ballater)	147

Handicap

G.S. Middleton	(Murcar)	(8)	136

R.G.L. Davidson	(Ballater)	(9)	140
R.A. Cheyne	(Northern)	(4)	140
G.C. Farrington	(Ballater)	(12)	140

Gordon Farrington came to Ballater from Littlestone, Kent and is now Head Greenkeeper at Royal Dublin.

1987.

S. Davidson	(Northern)	147
F.G. Gray	(Murcar)	149
A. Howie	(Hazlehead)	150

Handicap prizes were shared by four players who each returned 141. They were N. Meldrum (Hazlehead), R. Cattenach (Edzell), G.R. Sherrifs (Deeside) and R.L. Nicoll (Murcar). The best local scratch was John Pringle with 158. The local handicap winner was A. Michie (11) 143.

1988.

G.J. Mitchell	(Northern)	138
A. Cruickshank	(Hazlehead)	141
K. Leslie	(Torphins)	142

Handicap

| M. Mitchell | (Ballater) | (9) | 128 |
| A. Chivas | ,, | (18) | 137 |

1989

S. Henderson	(Bon-Accord)	135
J.F. Hardie	(Ballater)	138
Dr R.P. Ford	(Scotscraig)	141

Henderson's scores were 65 and 70. His 65 was considered a new course record since the sequence of holes had been altered.

Handicap

C. Fraser	(Royal Aberdeen)	(15)	123
C. Beaton	(Elgin)	(9)	131
G. McCombie	(Ballater)	(11)	134

1990.

J.G. Bochel	(Nairn)	145
J. Cramond	(Hazlehead)	146
W.G. Methven	(Royal Aberdeen)	146

Handicap

Iain Mitchell	(Ballater)	(15)	134
M. Stephen	(Hazlehead)	(8)	134
A.A. Mitchell	(Ballater)	(10)	135
J. Nimmo	,,	(7)	136

113

The Mitchells, son Iain and his father Alan do well!
1991.

John Cramond	(Hazlehead)		133
A. Cruickshank	(Caledonian)		145
G.Prise	(Murcar)		146

Handicap

Iain Mitchell	(Ballater)	(13)	123
F.G. Gray	(Murcar)	(5)	133
D. Cameron	(Deeside)	(10)	133

John Cramond winning for the second time had a record breaking aggregate of 133. In 1959 Innes Wright had completed the shorter course in 131.

Iain Mitchell had the best handicap score for the second year running and promptly had his handicap cut to 10. His aggregate was not a record—it equalled the net scores of P. Simon (18–Batchwood St Albans) in 1984, and C. Fraser (15—Royal Aberdeen) in 1989. His performance next year will be watched with interest—but that's another book!

There were 64 single-figure golfers (somewhat more than half the field), yet only one player scored less than 70 (he did it by a margin). The course was in beautiful condition and the weather was fine. Maybe it's not such an easy course after all.

Finally to wind up this review of the Ballater Open let it be recorded here that Walter McLennan in 1991 at the age of 70 completed two rounds in nets of 68 and 69 (off 17) to beat all other Ballater members (except Iain Mitchell) in the handicap. The CSS was 69 all day. A few days later Walter now playing-off 14 was second in the over-60's Murray Cup and again played to his handicap.

*   *   *

Tournaments like the Open do not just happen. They have to be organised year after year. Bert Ingram is now a dab hand at that. But the starting (and collecting of money), the recording of scores, the selling of raffle tickets, and the sensible parking of cars requires the assistance of willing volunteers. Among those who have given their time year after year have been Leslie Sandison, Sandy Coutts, George Duguid (and beware of driving off before he has given the signal to strike!), Bill Hardman, John Brough, the late Ted Clark, and many others, including, of course, many of the ladies.

ELEVEN

Other Club Competitions and the Trophies

In the 1890's not many meetings are held and there are few mentions of golf or competitions. However at a meeting in May 1896:

... Mr Humphreys suggested that a medal be given and played for in June, July, August and September; the competitors to be handicapped and the player having the lowest aggregate at the end of the season to be the winner.

In July 1898:

John Simpson said that he had been informed by Sir Allan MacKenzie that Lady MacKenzie wished to present the Club with a cup. It was resolved to accept the cup and the Secretary was instructed to write and thank Lady MacKenzie.

The Club's Medal was won in 1898 by William A. Duguid. Recording this in the minutes the Secretary added that a Medal would be played for in 1899. The Committee also decided to have cards printed giving 'scale of charges, a sketch of the course, the lengths of the holes and that they be put into the hotels and principal lodging houses'.

At a meeting in April 1900 it was reported that Mr George Grant had won the Club Medal and Mr Wilcox the Lady MacKenzie Cup.

By the summer of 1902 there were three cups:

The Gray-Warner cup	July
The Lady MacKenzie cup	August
Dr George Ogilvie's cup	September

The first mentioned had been presented by a Mr Alex Gray and a Mr Warner of Aberdeen.

In early June 1904 the Handicap Committee agreed the following fixture list for the season:

June	14	Club's medal
,,	21	Mr Robb, the Jeweller's cup
,,	28	Lady MacKenzie's cup
July	12	Club's medal
,,	21	Visitors' competition
,,	26	Dr Ogilvie's cup
August	9	Club's medal
,,	18	Visitors' competition
,,	26	Ladies match
September	6	Club's medal
,,	15	Visitors' competition

It was arranged that visitors play for handicap one week previous to the dates mentioned above for their competitions.

The Ogilvie Cup was won for the second time in succession by William Beekie in July 1905 (82−2=80) and became his property. The Ogilvie Cup, then, disappears from Club affairs. (see appendix Four for a note about the remarkable Ogilvie's).

Prior to the official opening of the extended course on 16th August 1906 a Medal was played on 1st August:

W.J. Thomson	88−8=80
Wm. Beekie	90−8=82
H.S.F. Jebb	94−10=84
John Hanna	96−12=84
Allan Smith	98−10=88
David Birrell	99−10=89
J.D. Littlejohn	101−10=91

The Free Press 8th September 1906 shortly after the 18 hole course had been opened:

Ballater Club. Play for the Club's medal took place over the Ballater course on the 4th inst., when the following four gentlemen tied for 1st place with nett scores of 81 each, viz: Colonel Gordon, Messrs H.S.F. Jebb, John Proctor, and F.J. Smith. The ties were played off on Friday when the subjoined cards were handed in: Mr John Proctor 89−10=79; H.S.F. Jebb 90−10=80; Colonel Gordon 96−9=87; F.J. Smith 100−8=92.

The Jebb Cup

Initially known as the Captain's Cup the name was changed to the Jebb Cup at the A.G.M. in 1909. Presented by H.S.F. Jebb in 1907. The conditions he stipulated are set out in the minutes of a meeting held on 18th June 1907:

116

The cup to be called the Captain's prize; to be played for in August; that it can never, under any circumstances, be kept by anyone, however many years in succession they may be successful; the winner will hold the cup for one year, and at his own expense have his name and the year engraved on it.

The fate of the Ogilvie Cup may well have persuaded Jebb that this could not happen to his. The winner is now decided by match play between the top 16 qualifiers in a Winter season medal.

The Yarrow Trophy

In July 1911 F.J. Yarrow presented a Silver Ink Stand for Annual competition. The Committee decided that the conditions should be:

Stroke competition 36 holes on two dates, 18 holes on each, total of the two scores to count. The winner to receive a prize value 15/- and have his name engraved on the stand. The Ink Stand to remain in the Pavilion for use.

The first winner was the Club Captain, H.S.F. Jebb. The last winner engraved on the trophy was Ian Paterson in 1978. He won after a play-off with Ian Simpson and Davie Morrison. Since then the handsome trophy has been resting in the showcase. (See Vic Shepherd Cup below.)

Fred J. Yarrow, was a coal exporter to South America, and he and his wife, and his children and grandchildren holidayed in Ballater for many years.

At first they lived at Newton of Gairn, then at Monaltrie House (they moved because Mrs Yarrow complained that it was too windy at Newton), finally moving back to Newton which they used until 1939. After Fred died (in 1928) his son, Ernest, who had built Balanreich, moved to Monaltrie. Dr Dudley Yarrow and Freddie Griffith-Jones, grandsons of Fred Yarrow live in Sevenoaks and Little Missenden respectively.

Fred Yarrow donated the cost of the installation of electric lighting and an electric organ blower at St Kentigern's Church in 1919 and 1920.

The Club Championship

72 holes stroke play over four days around the third week in June. Usually Sunday, Tuesday, Thursday and Saturday.

The Ballater Open

36 holes. Played first Saturday in August. First played in 1931. Since 1950 the winner has received the Lochnagar Shield donated by Captain Frai. The Jungle Cup—handicaps 1–9.

McLean Cup

Presented to the Club by James McLean of Craigendarroch in 1952 to be awarded to the winning pair in a mixed foursomes match-play com-

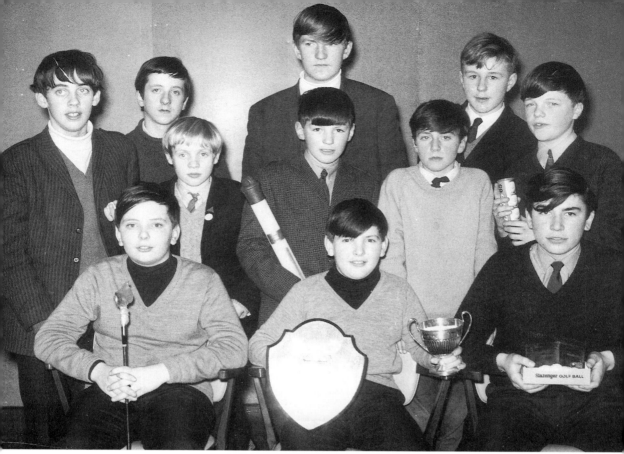

The five in the back of this group of young golfers are G.W. Richmond, A. Grigor, Stewart Archibald, Barry Steel, and Philip Fraser. The middle group of three are A. Smith, Philip Massie, and W. Johnston. In the front are Euan Hardman, Donald Hardman, and Robert Petrie.

petition. The leading sixteen from a Mens medal and from a Ladies medal qualify for the match-play stages. There is a draw for partners. In the mid-Fifties the McLean family were substantial Hoteliers, son Richard in the Craigendarroch Hotel, Walter, the other son ran the Fife Arms Hotel in Braemar. The family moved to New Zealand in 1958.

The Craigendarroch Cup
Presented by James McLean in 1974. Mens foursomes match-play. Draw for partners.

The Riverside Trophy
Presented, in 1977, by Alan and Ella Robertson who have presented a prize to the winners and the runners-up since the competition was introduced. Mixed foursomes, match-play, for married couples.
Alan Robertson is from Torphins. Alan and Ella came to Ballater in 1937 when he was appointed manager of the Riverside Garage, then

118

owned by Colonel Milne. In 1939 the garage was taken over by the Army and filled with stores (clothing mainly) in preparation for the ill-fated Norwegian campaign in 1940. Unfortunately the garage (and its contents) was destroyed by fire and Alan subsequently bought the remains from Colonel Milne. He re-built it in 1950/51 and ran it until his retirement in 1978.

From the rear of their Golf Road house the Robertsons have a beautiful view over the course towards Craig Vallich. Their back garden is the main gathering (and collection) point for the hooked ball off the 18th Tee!

The Duffus Cup

Presented by J.C. Duffus of Riverstone House. John Coutts Duffus, an Edinburgh stockbroker, and his wife Wendy joined the Club in September 1965. They now live in Aberdeen. Mrs Duffus' parents had lived in Gordon Cottage on the Green. Separate medals producing 16 qualifiers for a mixed foursomes 18 hole medal, (draw for partners). The first winners of the cup were Mrs D. Todd who was partnered by W.G. Richmond.

Royal Deeside Golf Week Silver Salver

Presented by the participants in the first Golf Week which was held in 1975. Similar to the McLean and Duffus Cups except that the sixteen mixed pairs drawn together (following a qualifying medal) play a Greensomes medal over 18 holes.

[The fact that in the three mixed foursomes competitions mentioned above the pairs are decided by draw led to a suggestion that there should be a competition open to those who live together or who wish to live together—but the Council of the day was unmoved.]

The Mary Hynd Trophy, The Fraser Cup, The St.Nathalan Cup

These are all scratch match-play. The Mary Hynd (Scratch to 9) being presented, in 1974, by Donald Hynd, a former Captain, in memory of his late wife, the Fraser Cup was also presented in 1974 (10 to 18) by Jim Fraser, and the St Nathalan Cup in 1985 (19 to 28) by Bert Mutch, Secretary of the Lodge.

Provost Anderson Trophy

Presented in 1970 by Willie Anderson a Ballater man whose father lived in Aberdeen Cottage. Anderson, a very keen golfer, was Match Secretary for a time. He settled in a Banking position overseas. 36 holes stableford.

Vic Shepherd Cup

Born in 1918, Vic died in 1978. Victor Shepherd was apprenticed at his brother's hairdresser shop in Bridge Street, Ballater in the thirties.

After the war he worked in Jon's the hairdresser in Bridge Street, Aberdeen, until in 1960 he and his brother Bob bought an established hairdressers, Pat Grants in Crown Street. He was a fine, enthusiastic golfer and, even when working in Aberdeen, would drive out to Ballater in the early evening to take part in the mid-week competitions. His most famous feat was to score consecutively, 3, 1, 2 over todays 12th, 13th, and 14th holes. He was a member of Murcar Golf Club for many years. At his request his ashes were scattered on the old 9th green on the Ballater course.

In September 1979 the Council decided that the Vic Shepherd Cup should replace the Yarrow Trophy which had become tarnished with age and it was thought best to lay it to rest in the display cabinet. The competition is a 36 hole medal.

The Philip Trophy
Presented in 1985 by Andrew A.B. Philip C.A. of Aberdeen who, like others, 'just wanted to put something back'. He has happy memories of childhood holidays in Ballater and still weekends or holidays in his house close to the golf course. The competition is an eighteen hole four ball better ball stableford. Draw for partners.

The Pringle Cup
Presented in 1970 by John Pringle, father of John, (former Captain), Robert (of the Garage), and Kathleen Anderson. Thirty six holes stroke play.

Veteran's Trophy
Match-play for the over 50's. First played for in 1963.

Murray Cup
Presented in 1974 by Aberdonian Ernest Murray (who also presented the Yarrum Cup for Junior match-play). Enthusiastic golfer and humourist. Ballater Antiques dealer. Eighteen holes medal.

Jamieson Trophy
Presented in 1973 by Alfred J. Jamieson who at one time lived at Corby Hall on the Abergeldie estate. He and Ed Stuart became friends and Ed made more than one visit to Jamaica to tend Jamieson's garden. Thirty six holes Stableford for the over seventies. The first winner was Ed Stuart.

Corrybeg Trophy
Presented by Matt Michie in 1974. The ruins of Corrybeg can be found beyond Craggan on the Dinnet (formerly Morven) estate. Corrybeg was farmed by Matt's grandparents. Eighteen holes foursome stroke-play. Alan Robertson and Harry Wright were the first winners.

120

ABOVE *In the 1970's the Ballater team of Molly Godsman, Rosalind Roy, Peggy Sutherland (with Pennant), Gillian (Thain) Petrie, and Catriona (Hardman) Morrison won the Kincardine and Deeside Ladies Golf Pennant for the first time.*

ABOVE *Matt and Rose Michie with Ernest Murray celebrate with some 'finest hand-made English pewter'.*

Dr J.G. Moir, outdoor Curling enthusiast.

BELOW *Vic Shepherd*

BELOW *Jim Forbes Club Champion in 1980 and 1981.*

BELOW *Fred J. Yarrow*

Stuart Sutherland Memorial Rose Bowl
Presented by Peggy Sutherland in 1982 in memory of her husband a Ballater Painter and Decorator. Thirty six holes medal.

Provost Milne Trophy
Presented in 1975 by Colonel Milne of Invermuick (the old Manse) who was Provost of Ballater from 1919 to 1925. Eighteen holes Senior/Junior medal. First won by Alistair Cassie and R. Cooper.

The William John Roy Memorial Trophy
This trophy was presented to the Club in 1987 in memory of Bill Roy, who was killed in a motor accident in 1986 at the age of 41.
He was a native of Ballogie, Aboyne. He and his wife Rosalind came to Ballater in 1972.
Bill was an enthusiastic golfer and Committee member, who was always keen to represent the Club in competitions and matches, and had great pleasure as a supportive and involved member in all the social aspects of the Club. Bill's wife Rosalind dispenses a welcome dram to the participants in the competition which is a thirty six hole medal.

The Anderson Cup
Presented by Mrs H.G. Anderson in 1914 in memory of her husband, who was Club President from 1906 until his death in 1913. This is the only Bogey competition.

The Anderson Driver
This historic club was presented to Mrs Anderson on the occasion of the opening of the extended course in 1906. The club disappeared for a time but was found and recovered from an antique shop in Aberdeen! Winter match-play for sixteen qualifiers from a medal. Mr Willox supplied the club and a ball and was paid 17/- for the goods.

Rosebank Trophy
Presented in 1974 by Ian Paterson. It is the name of a house which Ian built and they occupied when they lived in Ballater. Winter medal competition—weather permitting! Eight rounds, four counting. Ian was Captain 1976 to 1979.

Medals
A Medal is played every month from March to November inclusive. Some of the Medals are also used as qualifying rounds for other competitions.

March	Hennessey qualifying
April	Rover Cup qualifying
June	R.N.L.I. Spoon
July	N.S.C.R. Prize

August	Whyte & Mackay
September	Anderson Driver qualifying
October	Jebb Cup qualifying

Craig-Coillich Shield

Presented in 1959 by Lewis Gillies, (of Riverside Garage and later the Victoria Street Garage) a Ballater Town Councillor. The shield is shared by the men and the ladies. The men have a play-off medal for the season's medal winners in October while the ladies award the shield to the player with the best aggregate score of the medals played from April to September.

Other Competitions

The Famous Grouse Shot-gun foursomes. This is for the men and is the only competition in which they can select their partner.

Open Charity Mixed foursomes. Bar-B-Q.

18 hole Open mixed. Sunday following 18 hole Open.

Captain's prize. Last Sunday in October.

R.S.P.C.C. Putter. Only two clubs and putter permitted.

The Ballater team which won the Aberdeenshire Ladies County Golf Association inter-club team stroke-play competition for the Watt Dufuss Trophy at Banchory in 1990: front — Sheena Gordon and Gillian Petrie, middle — Heather Backhouse and Margaret Joss. Behind is Mrs Carol Milne, President of A.L.C.G.A.

TWELVE

The Scott Trophy

This trophy was presented by Mr James Scott who was the Liberal M.P. for Kincardine and West Aberdeenshire from 1929 to 1931. It is competed for by teams of four drawn from clubs within the (then) constituency. The format is medal play with all scores counting.

From time to time various clubs (such as Braemar, Auchenblae, Laurencekirk, Lumphanan, Torphins, Tarland, and Portlethen from 1989) have entered teams, so far without success. So far the winners have been Banchory (22 wins), Stonehaven (16), Aboyne (11) and Ballater (5). The venue rotates between these four clubs plus Braemar, who were unlucky to lose a three hole play-off after a tie with Stonehaven in 1931.

Ballater did not enter a team in the first year but in 1930 the Club was represented by George Rezin, I.J. Findlay, C.A. Munro, and George Ironside. The venue was Banchory and the event was won by the home team, Ballater coming 4th (of 7). George Rezin had the lowest two-round total (144) beating W. Watt of Stonehaven by one shot. In 1935 Rezin again had the lowest two round total, this time at Banchory when his aggregate was 144. The home team won the competition and Dr Park, the Banchory Captain, presented the trophy.

In 1936 Mr C.M. Barclay-Harvey, who succeeded James Scott as M.P., presented a cup to be awarded to the player with the best aggregate score on the day. The first winner was W. Watt of Stonehaven with a total of 141 at Aboyne. George Rezin required a finish of 4 3 3 in the morning for a 67 after being out in 32 but he had a disastrous 7 at the 16th. In the afternoon Rezin took three putts on the last green and thus failed by one stroke to tie with Watt. In the meantime F.K. Gordon of Aboyne was having a remarkable finish of 3 2 3 2 3 to his afternoon round of 69 but this only enabled his team to tie with Stonehaven who won the play-off.

1951—Ballater's first win in the Scott Trophy. On the left Norman Thain (winner of the Barclay-Harvey cup), Alan Gibb and George Rezin (holding the trophy). The fourth member of the team was Ian Phillips.

The following year, at Ballater, Rezin tied on 146 but lost the five hole play-off by two strokes to J.K. M'kay of Aberdeen University and Aboyne who finished two under fours. The match was refereed by Sir Malcolm Barclay-Harvey the donor of the individual cup. Ballater finished fourth behind Stonehaven.

In the remaining years of the thirties, when they played, (the Club couldn't raise a team in 1938 or 1939) Ballater returned average scores and arrived at World War 11 without a win.

The competition started up again in 1949 but it wasn't until 1951, playing at home, that Ballater, represented by George Rezin, Dr Alan Gibb, Norman Thain, and Ian Phillips, had their first win, and it was Norman, in his prime, who won the Barclay-Harvey Cup (the Cup) with a total of 149, a shot ahead of George Rezin and Norman Hinks of Banchory.

In 1952 Innes Wright (139) won the Cup at Aboyne to lead Aboyne to victory. He won again in 1953, 1955 and 1962.

In 1957 Ian Clark tied with Norman Hinks for the Cup but came second after a three hole play-off.

Alistair McGregor won his first Cup in 1965 with rounds of 68 and 65 at Banchory. His second came in 1967 when his aggregate was 149 at Ballater but Banchory won the Cup. Then in 1969 he regained the cup with rounds of 69 and 68 at Stonehaven.

Ballater's second win came in 1972 when Alistair McGregor, his brother Fred McGregor, John Pringle, and Ian Mitchell playing at home

125

beat Banchory by one stroke.

In 1973 Alistair McGregor won the Cup for the fourth time, equalling the number won by Norman Hinks, and Innes Wright, but Ballater lost by a stroke to Banchory playing at Braemar.

A third win for Ballater came in 1977 when Ian Simpson, Fred McGregor, John Pringle and Ian Mitchell had a comprehensive win, all their scores being between 70 and 76.

In 1979 Jim Hardie playing for Ballater for the first time beat the field with 67 and 64 to win the Cup at Stonehaven.

In 1982 Ballater (at home) won for the fourth time playing Jim Hardie, John Pringle, Ian Simpson and Fred McGregor. Jim Hardie scored two 71's to win the Cup. In 1983 at Braemar, Hardie retained the Cup with rounds of 65 and 67.

Ballater's fifth win came in 1986 when John Pringle won the Cup with 143 at Aboyne. The other members of the winning team were Jim Hardie, Fred McGregor and R.G.(Bob) Petrie (Centenary year Captain). In the following year Fred McGregor won the Cup with a score of 146 at Ballater.

In the final year in this review, 1991, the competition was played at Aboyne where some of the new holes (notably the 15th and 16th) caused problems and scoring was somewhat higher than in former years.

Since 1931 49 different players have represented Ballater. The selection honours go to the McGregor brothers who between them have played on 34 occasions—Alistair has played 15 times since 1957 and Fred has played 19 times since 1969. Norman Thain played on 13 occasions and Jim Hardie has just equalled that number.

BELOW *Three members of a Ballater team—Ian Phillips, Norman Thain and Tom Forbes with the starter at Stonehaven.*

THIRTEEN

The Royal Deeside Golf Week

The idea of a Deeside Golf Week was first mentioned in March 1958 when the Captain, A.J. Todd, gave a report to the Council of a meeting of the Tourist Association. It had been decided to ask the Golf Clubs on Deeside to run a tournament during the month of May in which the competitors would play one round each on the Banchory, Aboyne, Ballater, and Braemar courses. Ballater Golf Club had been asked to take the lead in the arrangements. The Council decided to ask the other Clubs to send representatives to a meeting to be held on 21st March. The Club was to be represented by Alec Todd, Mr Anderson, Mr Smith, and the Secretary. The Ladies section was asked to send representatives. There is no further reference to this combined Club meeting, nor indeed to the idea of a multi-club Golf Week. But the minutes of the meeting held immediately after the A.G.M. on 27th March 1974 include:

> The Captain Mr J.D. Hynd informed the Committee about a meeting he had held with Miss Judith Sleigh (Grampian Tourist Association), Mr Chillas, Mr Mitchell, and Mrs Simpson. The idea Miss Sleigh put forward was for a Golf Week in Ballater. It was agreed to discuss the matter with Hoteliers, the Ballater Businessmen's Association and the Town Council.

At this meeting Ian Paterson, as spokesman for the Town Council, said they would be willing to donate a trophy to be played for during the Golf Week and the Town Council would give a Civic reception for the visitors. The Golf Club would become a member of the Grampian Tourist Association.

In November the Captain, Mr J.D. Hynd reported that Elliot Rowan and J. Wilson of Pitlochry had agreed to attend. Help had been received from Mr L.M. Kerr, Captain of the Nairn Golf Club, in obtaining the services of Elliot Rowan.

The first Golf Week, held from 4th to 10th May 1975, was an undoubted success, the result of the tremendous enthusiasm of all those connected with it.

Judith Sleigh produced a report which was discussed by the Council who thought it was so good and so comprehensive that it should be used as a guide in organising the 1976 Golf Week.

Donald Hynd informed the Council that the Grampian Tourist Board were not prepared to help to the same extent again but they would underwrite any losses. He proposed that the Golf Week Committee should comprise of members of the Golf Club, one Hotelier, one member of the Ballater Businessmen's Association and that Colonel Napier and George Smith should be asked to call a meeting of their respective bodies to appoint a representative. Hynd wrote to the Professionals inviting them for next year and asking about their fees.

A working Committee was formed consisting of — Harry Wright, Bill Hardman, Ian Paterson, A. Robertson and B. Schmidt. Alister Cassie suggested that Golf Week 1976 be advertised in *Golf Monthly*.

The Royal Deeside Golf Week (as it became known) was soon established as a popular event in The Ballater Golf Club year. There were plenty of volunteers to help, particularly during the Week. Many members have dedicated time and work to the week over the years since 1975 including Rupert and Eileen Macnamee, Matt and Rose Michie, Bill Hardman, a succession of Captains (not least Donald Hynd who was a tower of strength in the first year of the event), Rosalind Roy, Alister Cassie, George Smith, Harry Wright, John Brough, George Duguid, the late Gordon Kinghorn, Leslie Sandison and of course, Bert and Irene Ingram, and many others.

The programme has remained substantially the same over the years:

Saturday: Arrival and registration. Visitors are welcome to play in the 'Sweepers'—Ladies 11.45 a.m. Men 12.45 p.m. In the evening there is a reception and dance at the Clubhouse.

Sunday: In the morning, a Greensome competition, tuition by the Professionals, and a bus tour for the non-golfers. In the evening Country and Western in the Clubhouse.

Monday: Stableford competition and Long Driving competition on the 2nd hole. Tuition and bus tour. In the evening Whist and a showing of films of local interest.

Tuesday: Medal—first round. Tuition and bus tour. 'Taste of Scotland' night in the Clubhouse including cabaret and Scottish Country Dancing.

Wednesday: Inter-Hotels, Seniors and Bowling competitions. Bridge or

128

A group of 1991 Royal Deeside Golf Weekers with Leslie Sandison, Rose Michie, Margaret Joss and Bert Mutch (with the Texan neck-tie) in the rear.

Darts in the evening.

Thursday: Medal—second round. Tuition and bus tour. Ceilidh.

Friday: Mixed Foursomes and Professional's demonstration. In the evening prize-giving and farewell dance.

The average charge for the week in 1990 was £250—the price depending on the hotel selected. The tariff is for seven nights, dinner, bed and breakfast (including VAT) and covers golf, tuition, and entertainments. Non-golfers are charged approximately 10% less.

The Royal Deeside Golf Week at Ballater has been a great success since it started in 1975. In 1991 174 visitors (including 11 non-golfers) stayed in 15 Ballater Hotels and they had come from 82 different Golf Clubs. A high proportion of them place deposits for the next year before leaving Ballater at the end of the week—a measure of its popularity.

129

FOURTEEN

Club Secretaries

In August 1892 John McGregor, the Tenant of the Invercauld Arms Hotel and farm and a founder member of the Club, became its first secretary. He was followed in 1895 by John Lawson, the School-teacher and also a founder member. For the next fourteen years there were frequent changes and unfortunately research, so far, has not revealed much about the occupations of the following:

1896 David Morgan. (Banker?)

1900 William Willox the cycle agent.

1902 Tom Lambert jointly with F.W. Humphries. The records show that Tom Lambert's address was the Schoolhouse. In his letter (from Yorkshire) to John Beaton regretting that he was unable to attend the Braid/Vardon match luncheon in August 1906 Lambert wished the event success and good weather adding 'Keep Braid sober until after the match'!

1906 John Beaton. North Bank.

1907 Alick S. Melvin.

1908 John Beaton.

1908 Dr Profeit. Captain 1911 to 1913.

1909 John Hanna. Sergeant Major Hanna was born in 1862. He died in 1936, aged 74. He came from Rathkeale (the name he gave to the house he built in Ballater), near Limerick in Ireland. The house was subsequently re-named Arisaig. The first mention of Hanna is in the minutes of a Club meeting held on 30th November 1905 when his attendance is recorded. In 1907 at the age of 45 he was elected to the Club Council. In 1908 he was appointed Caddiemaster, with power to discipline the caddies for mis-conduct, and Ranger with sole powers to give orders to Greenkeepers and others working on the course. He became Secretary in May 1909 and was re-appointed annually for the

John Hanna with his wife, four daughters and Willie.

Bert Ingram at bay in his office surrounded by electronic equipment but with a fine view of the car park!

next 23 years. During the Great War, with Hanna away on duty, Dr Profeit acted as Secretary until, in 1915, he was himself called away to a Military Hospital. Mr J. Low then acted as temporary secretary assisted by Hanna's daughter Mary until her father returned in 1919.

In 1931 for the first time other names were put forward for the position and a ballot was held. Hanna's proposer was J. Keiller Greig and he was re-appointed. In 1932 he did not stand for election.

Older members remember his piercing whistle when summoning caddies to work or warning youngsters (whom he encouraged to roam around the course with one club using any ball they could find) to clear

131

off when members approached.

Dr Dudley Yarrow recalls being reprimanded by Hanna for playing tennis (on the Yarrow private court!) on a Sunday afternoon in the Twenties.

1932 W. Lemmon.

1946 A.B. Anderson. Clydesdale Bank. Alexander Buchan Anderson was Club Treasurer from 1933, when he became Manager of the Clydesdale Bank, Ballater, until 1948 when he moved to Aberdour. Prior to 1933 he had been with the Bank in Aberdeen and Edinburgh. Sandy Anderson was born in Wigtonshire. He served with the Royal Artillery and was a prisoner of war in 1918. The move to Ballater quickly cured him of the asthma which had been induced by gassing during the war. During the 2nd World War he served in the Observer Corps.

Anderson could remember a time in the thirties when the Dee was frozen and there was Curling under the bridge for a spell of five weeks. In a conversation in the summer of 1990 he recalled the thunder sound of the ice cracking on the river. The subsequent thaw and floods changed the course of the river and one green was lost. He died during Christmas in 1990 at the age of 94.

1947 Harold M. Williams. Clydesdale Bank.

1952 James Hay. Clydesdale Bank.

1961 William Hardie. He was a coal clerk at the Depot adjoining the Station.

1968 Betty Simpson.

1975 Irene Ingram.

1976 Mrs Fedo.

1977 Ted Clark. When the extension to the Clubhouse was completed in 1978 a newspaper report included this:

> To keep a 'machine' the size of Ballater Golf Club running smoothly requires a full-time secretary and during the run-up to the official opening Ted Clark often wished there were thirty hours a day and nine days a week.
>
> Ted is an Aberdonian by birth and is well known in the Granite City as a former butcher and at Ballater as a former hotelier.
>
> He told me that the Club is very popular with visitors and there are even provisional bookings for bus parties as far ahead as summer 1979.

1984 Bert Ingram. Born and educated in Aberdeen Bert was the Senior Chief Technician in the Clinical Biochemistry Laboratory of Aberdeen University located in the Forresterhill Hospital compound. He worked there for 26 years before retiring. He and his wife Irene (who has also contributed a great deal to the Golf Club) came to live in Ballater in 1973.

Bert played cricket for Mannofield and St Ronalds in Aberdeen. A useful Seniors golfer.

132

FIFTEEN

Greenkeepers, Professionals and Stewards

From around the mid-1890's the Club employed greenkeepers, and then when James Anderson came from Edinburgh in 1905 the Club had a Greenkeeper/Professional. This lasted off and on until 1961 when the Club decided to advertise for and employ a greenkeeper —not a professional—in other words a Professional Greenkeeper.

Some of the earlier greenkeepers gave lessons and sold golf balls, clubs and so on, some just sold the merchandise.

The first greenkeeper named in the minutes is Alexander Anderson. In April 1898, however the following minute appears:

> The Greens committee had gone over the course with the green keeper and pointed out where new teeing grounds would require to be made but that the green keeper had raised objections to almost every proposal that was made, and that his conduct had been altogether so unsatisfactory they had needed to report the circumstances to a meeting of the Club.

They decided that it was necessary to advertise for another man and the Secretary was instructed to inform Alexander Anderson. As a result Robert Harper of Old Aberdeen was appointed but something must have gone wrong because by the middle of May, Alex Anderson has been re-appointed at his old wage of 21/-. Later that summer Anderson had a brush with 'Sluie' Mitchell and he was asked to write a letter expressing regret 'at having spoken ... in the manner he admitted

133

having done'. Subsequently Mitchell agreed to Anderson being re-appointed provided he obeyed the Greens committee instructions.

In April 1898 it was resolved:

> that the green keeper's regular duties should commence on 16th May and end on 30th September; that prior to 16th May he would be employed two days in each week to have the teeing grounds and path leading to the course put in proper order; that his working day should be from 9 a.m. until 6 p.m. with an hour in the middle of the day for dinner; that he should be on the ground again not later than 7 p.m. and remain until 9 p.m.; that he should not engage in play during working hours but diligently occupy his time in keeping the course in good condition and doing any necessary improvements under the direction of a committee consisting of the Captain [John Simpson], Mr Lawson, and the Secretary [D. Morgan].

In the summer of 1905 advertisements in *The Scotsman* produced 25 applicants. From these a selection of four was submitted to Mr Duncan at Royal Aberdeen. The recommendation was that Mr James H. Anderson of Braid Hills course, Edinburgh, be appointed. Anderson accepted at a wage of 25/- per week and a months notice on either side.

The Committee reviewed the situation in October. They decided to increase the greenkeeping staff from three to eight assistants and to employ twelve boys at 1/6 per day for stone gathering. They were to be supervised by Alex Alexander who was now employed as an assistant. James Anderson was also reviewing the situation and he recommended to the committee the following purchases: Five Cwt Hamilton manure. Two Bushels Stewarts Best Lawn Seeds (Putting Green). One 16" Pennsylvania Lawn Mower. 18 Flags. 20 Sand Boxes. One Hand Roller 24"×26" 4cwt Shanks. 40 Galvanised Tee Markers. 18 Cups for holes-—Cast iron bottoms. One Pick. One Grape. One Shovel.

The Club decided that the Greenkeeper should be allowed to teach and make and repair golf clubs it being understood that the work was not to interfere with his duties as Greenkeeper. They agreed that he could charge 2/6 a round and 1/- an hour, the fees to be shared equally with the Club.

There is no doubt that James Anderson did a good job for the Club and it must have come as a blow when he resigned in April 1908.

James Forbes was asked to take on the work. His hours were fixed 6 to 8 a.m. 9 to 1 p.m. and 2 to 5 p.m. Saturday off at 1 p.m. to receive instructions from the secretary.

1910 James Forbes, Ballater.
1910 William Porter (Assistant).
1911 Charles Forbes (extra greenkeeper).
1912 A. Anderson Greenkeeper for Bowling and Tennis.
1917 William Hanna, John Hanna's son.

Derek Livingstone head greenkeeper retires after 28 years tending the course, putting green, the bowls green and tennis courts. Dr Bill Manson (left), the Captain, makes the presentation on 14th July 1989. To the right are Matt Michie, Derek's wife Jean and the club's oldest member Ella Robertson.

1928 James Forbes, Ellwood (re-engaged).

March 1933 W. Michie.

April 1935 E. Christie of Stonehaven with Willie Hanna assistant.

In March 1949 the greenkeeper's hours, from the beginning of April to the end of September, were 7 a.m. to Noon. 1 p.m. to 5 p.m. on weekdays. Saturdays 7 a.m. to Noon. Two weeks holidays at the end of the season plus local holidays. Winter hours to be adjusted to make 44 per week over the year.

1949 E.W. Munro. Resigned in February 1951 to emigrate to New Zealand where some members have visited him.

1951 A. Benzie.

1953 Robert Troup engaged as assistant for five months.

1958 John Hardie. In 1959 he was given permission to sell balls, tees and other golf equipment but on terms which compensated the Club for its loss of revenue on these sales. He was to give the Club £50 or half his profit whichever was the less.

1961 John Hardie resigns and the Club decides to apply for a greenkeeper who will not have any responsibility for selling golf equipment or for teaching.

1961 Derek Livingstone retired in July 1989 having been head greenkeeper for twenty eight years. He left school at the age of thirteen to work for John Milne, the Grocer in Bridge Street (where the T.S.B. has its premises today). From 1942 he spent six years in the Royal Artillery (including service in Germany) before returning to Ballater as a milkman and then as assistant to Charlie Cumming on local services before becoming the greenkeeper.

He recalls with great enjoyment, the occasions during his early days as greenkeeper when the Secretary would hand him his pay envelope on a Friday and then recover the envelope so that it could be used next Friday, and next Friday. . . .

C. Michie was appointed as assistant greenkeeper on 15th January 1962 and he worked on the course until his resignation in 1976. He is the Janitor at the school.

1985 Gordon Farringdon. An early replacement for Derek Livingstone, he stayed a couple of years before moving on to Royal Dublin.

1988 Gordon Smith spent about a year at Ballater before moving to Liphook via St Andrews.

1989 Derek Cowan, who with his wife and family, has settled happily into the Ballater scene. Derek came from the Musselburgh Golf Club at Monktonhall, where he was head greenkeeper.

THE PROFESSIONALS

During the early years of the Club the Greenkeeper usually doubled as the Professional. James Anderson who had come to the Club in 1905 from Braid Hills fulfilled this role until his resignation in May 1908. The Club then advertised and W. Marr, who came from the Deeside Club was appointed as Professional from 1st June to 30th September 1908:

> ... wages 15/- weekly along with all coaching fees and with the privilege of selling golf material and repairing clubs. Duty to go over all the greens every morning and see that they along with the course are in good order for play....

The appointment was short lived because at the A.G.M. in 1909 it was agreed that no professional would be engaged for the following season.

At a Council meeting held in April 1961 it was announced that John Hardie had resigned as Greenkeeper and Professional.

However it wasn't until the Club was 80 years old that the Council, under the Captaincy of J.D. Hynd, decided that the Club should have a full time Professional.

A meeting in July 1973:

> Mr J.M. Stark, Secretary of the Scottish Section of the P.G.A. and Professional at Crieff, attended.... He had looked over the course and studied last year's balance sheet.... Mr Stark stated that in order to obtain the services of a good man it would be necessary for the Club to pay a retaining fee of about £750 a year, and in addition erect a lockfast, insurable shop and workroom of about 30'×15'. On the credit side the Club would have the benefit of a Professional who would provide the following services to Club members and visitors:
>
> ... a well stocked shop, golf lessons, a repair service, encouragement and instruction of junior members, starter for visiting parties and Club competitions, advice on course architecture, administration of course discipline, organisation of inter-club matches, welcoming visitors and establishing good relations with them, sale of tickets for golf, tennis, putting, and bowls.

A general meeting of the Club was held in August 1973:

> There were 38 members present. The Captain introduced J.M. Stark who then repeated his earlier presentation winding up with the promise that the P.G.A. would advertise in its Journal, vet applicants, and provide a shortlist to the Club for final decision.

In the event John Chillas was appointed the first full-time Professional to the Club in November 1973. He stayed until April 1975. In 1976 he became the professional at Crow Wood Golf Club, Glasgow, before moving to Stirling, and on to Glenbervie in 1991.

Chillas was followed by Ronnie McDonald who turned professional in 1971. Ronnie was assistant to Harry Bannerman at Banchory before joining Ballater where he stayed for four years, leaving in September 1979 in order to play more tournaments. Later he spent some time at

Deeside, and the Kings Links, Aberdeen before opening a golf shop in Aberdeen. In 1991 he took up a new job as professional at Westhill.

David Scott, of the Ardeer Golf Club, in Ayrshire joined Ballater on 1st February 1980 and stayed until February 1981.

In April 1981 Gary Dornan replaced Scott.

Fraser Mann joined Ballater in 1986 and stayed through 1991 before leaving to join his brother Lindsay (who played Walker Cup golf as an amateur) in starting up the Carnoustie Golf Centre, in the High Street of their home town. Fraser intends to devote more time in 1992 to the Tartan Tour—an activity which he has had to restrict while building up his business in Ballater.

Fraser spent 1982 and 1983 on the European Tour and has been the Scottish under-25 and assistants champion.

Lee Vannet who was one of Fraser's assistants (another was Sarah

Handover: Fraser Mann (left) greets his successor Joe Blair.

MacLennan now at East Sussex National) made several appearances in the Volvo European Tour in 1991.

Replacing Fraser Mann at Ballater in March 1992 will be Joe Blair who is from Prestwick originally but has spent the last ten years in Belgium. In recent years he has been with George Will, the well known Scottish Ryder Cup professional, at Royal Waterloo.

STEWARDS

In 1947 A.W. Leonard was appointed steward. He resigned in March 1955 and was made an honorary member for his services to the club. Thereafter there was a succession of stewards—Andrew M. Pithie (1955), Gordon Littlejohn (1956), James S. Duncan (1957), R. Troup, Alex Nixon (1964), W.G. Richmond (1969), Ean Grant, (1972), A. Cooper (1974), Adam Duguid (1977), until finally in 1978 stability arrived on the scene with the appointment of Yorkshireman, Martin Holroyd.

A keen walker and climber Martin Holroyd came to Ballater in April 1978 having spent six years in the Fife Arms Hotel in Braemar. He had previously worked as a Dispensing Optician in Bradford. He was a member of the Braemar Mountain Rescue Team for fifteen years until his recent retirement from active duty. He is now the Call Out Officer —responsible for mustering the Team.

Holroyd is also the secretary of the Ballater Angling Club. The members fish for Brown Trout in Invercauld's Loch Vrotachan nestling high up (2360 feet) in the hills behind the Cairnwell ski slopes. The Club is also allowed the use of Loch Muick at certain times (it's on the Balmoral estate), and a couple of small lochs on the Glen Muick estate.

Martin Holroyd – Steward

SIXTEEN

Royal Connections

The first mention of Balmoral is contained in the letter written by Sluie Mitchell to the Invercauld Factor, Mr Smith on 14th March 1905, when he mentions that he has heard that they (the Golf Club) 'are to let the grass to Mr Troup'. This 'Troup' was the gardener of the Royal Gardens, Balmoral Castle and Mitchell was confusing him with Troup the Butcher who was subsequently allowed to graze his sheep on the course. However in a letter dated 18th March 1905, the secretary wrote to Mr Troup at Balmoral asking what kind of seed he would recommend for permanent pasture on a golf course.

A minute dated 27th September 1905 records that The Duchess of Connaught (wife of the Duke of Connaught, third son of Queen Victoria), her daughter Princess Patricia, and Miss Pilley 'had this day patronised the course'. Following a discussion the Secretary together with Messrs Smart and Beaton was instructed to draw up a letter to forward to General Sir Dighton Probyn V.C., who was Keeper of His Majesty's Privy Purse, Balmoral Castle, asking him to use his good offices to induce His Majesty King Edward to grant permission to use the word 'Royal' in connection with the Club's title.

The letter was duly drawn up and despatched together with 'an explanatory circular'. Unfortunately no trace of the the circular can be found. At the next Council meeting (5th October 1905) the Secretary read a letter from the General in which he was commanded by the King to say that His Majesty did not feel justified at present in recommending that the Ballater Golf Club should be accorded the prefix 'Royal'.

The minutes of a meeting of the committee held on 30th July 1906 record:

A letter from Major Malcolm Murray, Equerry to H.R.H. Duke of Con-

140

naught was read intimating that H.R.H. Duchess of Connaught had graciously consented to honour the proposed Bazaar of 1907 with her patronage.

Vivien Saunders was one of the teaching Professionals at the Royal Deeside Golf Week in 1975 and 1976. She remembers visiting Balmoral and seeing the small golf course:

> The piece of information came back to me like a flash ... I was lucky enough to buy my own course at Abbotsley and was confronted by a gentleman who was about to become the men's Captain. He obviously felt that it was ridiculous that a woman should own a golf course and shouted at me 'tell me another woman who owns a golf course' to which I responded 'the Queen has a perfectly nice one at Balmoral'. I rather think that is the only thing the Queen and I have in common, other than the fact she was a patron of the P.G.A. when I was the only lady member and as such we were both entitled to wear the P.G.A. tie (there not being a head scarf)!

Ed Stuart was head gardener at Balmoral from 1951 until he retired in 1974. He was born in Bieldside, Aberdeen in 1902. Following an apprenticeship he became gardener to Sir Arthur Grant at Monymusk in 1925, then Lord Sempill at Fintray and Craigievar. In 1928 Ed was appointed Journeyman Gardener at Balmoral. He served in the R.A.F. from 1940 to 1945 as a P.T. Instructer.

In his best golfing days Ed had a single figure handicap at Ballater; at Balmoral, a course which could be said to have been designed to accommodate his skills, he was feared even when playing off +4! Ed died in 1990 at the age of 88.

An unidentified newspaper journalist writing in a local paper some years ago:

> But the sun did shine when I went down to Balmoral Castle to look up Ed Stuart, the head gardener ... it made the castle's nine hole golf course yell for a grooved swing.
>
> Reminded me of the time Ed and I did the circuit—and he finished in his best ever score of 29 ... Believe me it takes a golfer to do that—and it takes a golfer to win the cups Ed has collected over the years—it also takes a game with a head gardener to get you into the habit of replacing the divots!

In 1989 one of the Queen Mother's chefs holed out in one at the 13th playing in a 'sweeper'.

In September 1991 Prince Andrew played eighteen holes (pulling his own trolley) with Fraser Mann. Fraser confirms that the Prince is a powerful golfer with considerable potential—given the opportunity to play.

141

MATCHES WITH BALMORAL

In May 1929 it was suggested that an approach be made to Major MacKenzie at Balmoral asking if he would be agreeable to having matches at Balmoral and Ballater. There was a delay before the first match was played at Ballater in 1931 — the home team winning by five matches to one.

Ballater		Balmoral	
G.M. Rezin and J.L. Trotter	0	Capt. Ross and J. Edwards	1
Col. Stewart and A. Logan	1	W. Morrison and J. M'Gregor	0
D.C. Logan and J.W. Brockie	1	D.G. Watson and F. M'gregor	0
G. Leith and J. Rothney	1	J. Abercrombie and C. Asher	0
J. Findlay and C.W.A. Young	1	A. Stuart and E. Stuart	0
J. Robertson and W. Rowell	1	R. Chalmers and D.I.G. Gordon	0
	5		1

Of the less familiar names in the Ballater team J. Rothney was the Police Sergeant, Young and Robertson were bankers, and Rowell, a well-known singer, was in Customs and Excise.

The Balmoral team included Captain Ross, the Factor (formerly in Customs and Excise), Willie Morrison who was the grieve at one of the farms, J. McGregor, a Balmoral gamekeeper, whose piping skill made him famous, D.G. Watson was the Balmoral stonemason, J. Abercrombie was the head stalker, and Sandy Stuart, Ed's brother, was head gardener at Balmoral until he died around 1949 when Ed took over. The matches continued through the thirties the last pre-war one being that held on August 18th 1939 at Ballater. This was an all-day match with ten-a-side singles in the morning followed by five foursome matches after lunch, Ballater winning by ten to four on the day.

After the war there was an all-day match at Balmoral in September 1946 when the Royal Household Golf Club won by 9 matches to 4.

Thereafter there is no doubt that matches were held but successive Club Councils paid less and less attention to recording the results of any matches as opposed to Club competitions. Indeed for a time in the eighties hardly any records were kept. The arrival of the computerised print-out has solved this problem.

CRICKET

Harry Wright, the late Alexander (Bud) Fraser, a Balmoral Gillie, and Frank Banks the Balmoral 'Upholsterer' were mainly responsible for forming the post-war Crathie Cricket Club. Ballater has no regular cricket team nowadays but in past years golfers who were regular cricketers included Alec (Sandy) Grant, George Smith and his brother, Sandy, Ian Simpson, Dr J.G. Moir, Gordon Richmond, Davie Morrison,

Bill Roy, Stewart Davidson, Rupert Macnamee, D. and E. Hardman, and Gillespie Munro (who now teaches at Monymusk).

Dr Peter McEwan, a powerful member of the Crathie team remembers a match between the clubs in 1958 when, it seems, Harry Wright took 10 wickets for 23 runs. It was disappointing to hear McEwan go on to say that of course Crathie were playing 14 men that day against 15 from Ballater! Harry doesn't recall the occasion but it should be remembered that these matches were regarded as light-hearted fun and the 19th hole (in the form of the staff Mess) was a memory eraser.

The last match with the Golf Club (i.e. Ballater) took place in September 1975 when Crathie scored 204 for 6 Dec. (Willie Meston 63, Davie Morrison 25, Malcolm McEwan 22). The golfers mustered 93 (Gillespie Munro 57, Sandy Grant 26) and there were six ducks!

SEVENTEEN

The Bowls Club

The Bowling Green was constructed in 1907 the expenditure being mostly met from the surplus funds arising from the Bazaar. During the next forty years or so it is clear from the minutes of many meetings that the Bowling Club was considered a part of the Golf Club. The Club attended to the needs of the green and its surrounds and money was voted as required.

From time to time there are differences between the two committees but nothing very serious until in September 1948 the Club Committee met a deputation from the Bowling Club:

> Messrs Maitland, Richmond, and Copeland complained that the green had been neglected during the last month, and was practically unplayable. They reported that they had approached the greenkeeper to have the green cut closer but were refused. . . .
>
> They said they wished the green swept, mown, and rolled by Thursday 30th September when they were holding a Points Game.
>
> They also reported . . . it had been decided to approach the Golf Club with the suggestion that they take over the Bowling Green altogether and employ labour to keep the green in good order.

The Club Committee decided to employ Mr Logan, a retired Postman, to keep the green in order for two weeks until the end of the season. He was to be paid 2/3d per hour.

The committee also decided to refer the question of the Bowlers taking over the green to a general meeting of the Club. This was done at the half yearly meeting in November 1948 when after discussion it was decided that the committee should draw up an agreement in terms of the resolution which had been presented.

The terms were:

144

That the green be handed to the Bowling Club for a period of one year rent free. It was to be left to the Bowling Club to make their own arrangements regarding subscriptions, green fees, issue of tickets, labour and general management of the bowling green and surrounds. The Bowling Club to be responsible for the up keep of the Green which must be maintained in good condition. The Golf Club will [provide] the implements necessary ... the Bowling Club to be responsible for (their) maintenance. The Bowling Club to be responsible for their own financial arrangements, but it is understood that if, notwithstanding good management, a loss is incurred, the Golf Club undertakes to be responsible for any sum not exceeding twenty five pounds.

At the A.G.M. the following year (1951) it is felt that the trial year has been a success and it is suggested that the committee should now be empowered to grant a lease of, say, five years, with a possible break at three. This together with the question of a suitable rent to be discussed with the Bowling Club.

The meeting between the Bowlers and the Golfers took place in April the Bowlers being represented by Messrs Richmond, Maitland, and Copeland and Dr Middleton and the Club by Messrs Rezin, Todd, Williams (Secretary) and Dr Moir. George Rezin took the Chair.

At the end of the day the only real problem lay in the amount of rent. The Bowlers by their own efforts had acheived a great deal but their long term objective was a pavilion and they didn't see how this would be possible if they were burdened with a large rent. On the other hand they had not called upon the £25 reserved by the Club. The matter was referred back to the Club committee who after long discussion agreed that that a nominal rent of 1/- per annum be extracted from the Bowling Club in each of the next three years with the proviso that the Bowling Club's audited accounts be made available to the Golf Club.

The agreement was short lived for at a committee meeting in May 1952 the Captain, Dr Moir, reported that he had been approached by Dr Middleton, President of the Bowling Club, to find out whether or not the Golf Club Committee would be prepared to have the Golf Club staff look after the Bowling Green. The committee agreed to do the work for £2–15–0 weekly.

In April 1954 the rent payable to the Golf Club was increased to £5 per annum.

A Club Council meeting minute of 6th September 1954:

The attitude of members of the Bowling Club towards the Golf Club was mentioned and it was agreed that something should be done about it. Mr D.E. Smith proposed, seconded by Mr Adam, that the Bowling Club committee be asked to meet the Golf Club Council on Tuesday 14th September to discuss the relations. . . .

It's not clear if that meeting took place but at a council meeting that

145

day it was proposed that 'the subscription to be paid by the members of the Ballater Bowling club to be 10/- instead of £1'. This was approved at the half yearly meeting in October 1954 except that it is made clear that this applies only to non-playing members of the Golf Club.

The Captain also made a statement about the Bowling Club. He said that he had recently had a meeting with the Laird which arose because the Bowling Club had sent a deputation to the Laird requesting him to grant a Lease of the Bowling Green in order that they would have security of tenure before going ahead with erection of a pavilion. This was thought 'high-handed' since only the Golf Club could sub-let the Bowling Green. The Golf Club was itself negotiating a new Lease with Invercauld and it was decided to await events. The Bowling Club made its expected approach to the Golf Club in January 1955 and the Council agreed that once the Club's new Lease had been signed a Council meeting would be called to discuss the terms of the sub-lease.

The terms were to include annual rental of £12–10–0. The Bowlers were prepared to pay £10 and the argument went on until April 1956 when it was finally agreed that, in any case, the Club was prepared to waive the rent for the first two years. This was done to enable the Bowlers to spend money on improving the surrounds.

In 1957 the Bowling Club presented its proposals for the Pavilion and Gray and Kellas were asked to draw up an agreement. The Plans were submitted to the Club Council, accepted, and the agreement signed in early 1958. The Pavilion was duly constructed and there was a grand opening which was reported in the *Press*:

NEW £2200 PAVILION OPENED AT BALLATER

Big Day for Bowling Club

Ex-Baillie T.C. Smith, one of the founder-members of the fifty-year-old Ballater Bowling Club, was one of the large gathering at the club on Saturday to see a dream come true.

That was the opening of a £2,200 club pavilion which had its beginnings seven years ago by a donation of £5, and has had solid local financial support in fund-raising for the target over the years.

The president, Dr G.P. Middleton, commented on the support, when, in brilliant sunshine, he presided over the opening ceremony performed by Professor A.B. Stewart, Chair of Agriculture, Aberdeen University.

Among the guests were Mr Peter Craigmyle, Scottish Bowling representative; Mr V. Henderson, representing the contractors; Provost J.C. Begg and representatives of the Deeside and Donside Leagues, as well as golf and tennis representatives.

Dr Middleton said that great credit went to Mr T. Mochrie, Mr C. Copeland, and Councillor A.C. Paton, secretary for the work they had done towards getting the pavilion.

Professor Stewart recalled that he was born only a few miles from Ballater.

Mrs Middleton, wife of the president, officially opened the green by sending down the first jack and bowl.

Dr Middleton revealed that Mr Henderson, Scottish representative of the builders of the pavilion had donated a personal gift of an electric clock for the outside of the pavilion.

The building was decorated with a floral display by Captain P. Frai, and women members of the club provided refreshments.

The Bowlers, now with a fine pavilion, are still having money problems and in February 1960 they ask the Club to forego the rent for 1959. The Club declines to do this but agrees to carry it forward unpaid until such time as the Bowling Club could afford to pay it.

For the most part relations have remained good over the years since then, with the Golf Club recognising its responsibility for the Bowling Green but keeping a watchful eye on the expenditure required. Bert Mutch, President of the Bowling Club since 1990, represents the bowlers interests cogently at Club meetings.

Bert is probably better known as a golfer than as a bowler. He is a life member of the Bon-Accord Club, Aberdeen and, when travelling the world, ostensibly seeking work for his firm, he found time to collect over 300 score cards from clubs as far apart as Bangkok and Pebble Beach!

Bowling Club Pavilion — Opening Ceremony — 5th July 1958.
Inset: Pavilion committee: Left to right front. I. Brown, Dr G.P. Middleton,
President. A.C. Paton. Behind: Henry Nicol, C. Copeland, Tom Mochrie, J.
Smith.

EIGHTEEN

Consulting the Royal and Ancient

LATE ON THE TEE

The Minutes record that a meeting of the Handicap Committee was held on the evening of 10th October 1904 to consider the final of the Club's Gold Medal competition:

Mr Lawson proposed that the meeting find that Mr James Grant has won the medal and Mr Robert Davidson the second prize. Mr Willox seconded and the motion was carried unanimously.

That seems innocent enough but someone must have relayed the news to Mr Grant who immediately wrote to Mr Willox as follows:

Osborne House, Ballater

Gold Medal 1904

I have to hand notice of meeting tonight of Golf Handicap Committee, business the above Medal. On consideration of this matter I think it right that you should present the above to Mr Davidson who I have no doubt would have successfully won the Medal. Yours truly. James Grant.

In the meantime Tom Lambert, the Secretary, had written to Mr Davidson giving the Committee's decision, whereupon Mr Davidson replied as follows:

11th October 1904

Dear Sir,
Your note to hand and I may say that I am more than astonished at the

148

Committee's decision. How they make out that Mr Grant won the Medal and the final never played is past my comprehension; of course being an interested party I could not take it upon myself to attend the meeting but I consider that the Committee should have asked a written statement from us both and then if they considered that Mr Grant was entitled (not won) the medal I should certainly have accepted the second prize but as I consider that I have been very unfairly treated by the different actions I positively decline to accept any prize and I think the best course for your Committee to do, seeing Mr Grant could not wait for me the matter of nine minutes but at the same time waste a far longer period playing thirty-six holes, is give him both prizes. As I seem to be the only party who is in the wrong in the matter I consider it my duty not only to the Committee but to the Club in general to tender my resignation as a member of both Committees.

R. Davidson

P.S. I may here state that I could have refused to play at all not having any intimation from you that I was one of the finalists. [!]

This was not quite the end of the affair because in the meantime the Secretary had written to St Andrews requesting a ruling. The reply dated 6th December read:

The final (36 holes) of this Club's competition for gold medal is decided by holes, not strokes. A and B are the finalists. B not being in Ballater wires A that he will meet him at the first tee, ready for play, at a certain time. A turns up at the appointed time and waits fifteen minutes. At the end of this time, B not putting in an appearance, A commenced and played 16 holes alone when he was joined by the greenkeeper and together they played the remaining 20. The reason A started off without B was that he was afraid if he waited any longer there would not be sufficient daylight to enable him to play 36 holes. B comes on the course while A is playing No. 4 hole, and seeing A playing goes away again. A finished the 36 holes and handed in his card. B does not play at all. A second prize is given by the club to the runner-up. Has A won the medal and is B entitled to the second prize?

Answer—As the final is decided by holes, not strokes, A's score has no bearing on the case. If A was dissatisfied with B's non-appearance at the hour fixed, he could have lodged with the Committee in charge of the competition a claim to be declared the winner. It is the duty of the Committee to decide if B's explanation is satisfactory, and if not, to award the match to A. If the explanation is satisfactory, the Committee should fix a day and hour for A and B to play-off the final. The prizes to A and B, according to the decision of the Committee, or the result of the final, if played.

*   *   *

149

THE FLAGSTICK AFFAIR

8th July, 1936

The Secretary,
Ballater Golf Club.

Dear Sir,

With reference to the Club's Summer Competition the second round of which we played in this evening we wish to draw your attention to the following incident. Our approaches to the 7th green both of which landed on the green were played at what we supposed was the hole, and one ball lay about two feet from the flag. On our arrival at the green we found that the flag was not in the hole as it should have been placed by the previous players but stuck in the green in an upright position several yards away. This naturally spoiled the hole for both and at the same time upset our play for the succeeding holes.

While accepting the apologies of the members concerned, Messrs I. Findlay and D.E. Rezin, we desire the Committee under the circumstances to grant us permission to replay the round. In the meantime we have not returned cards for the course.

Yours faithfully,
W.G.M. Anderson
C.W.A. Young

The Secretary, W. Lemmon replied next day:

9th July, 1936

W.G.M. Anderson
C.W.A. Young.

Your letter will be placed before a Committee as soon as possible. In the meantime this competition will have to go on.

Your cards should have been returned with your scores irrespective of your complaint.

Yours,
W. Lemmon. Secretary

This brought an immediate response:

9th July, 1936

Dear Sir,

We have to acknowledge receipt of you letter 9th inst and note the matter will be placed before the Committee.

Our letter of 8th inst neither suggests nor is it our wish that the competition should not go on as originally intended, apart from our desire of a replay of the round.

We enclose the cards showing the respective scores for the round and would appreciate the Committee's decision prior to the close of the competition.

Yours faithfully,   W.G.M.A. and C.W.A.Y.

In the meantime the Secretary wrote to the Royal and Ancient, stating the facts as he saw them (unfortunately a copy of this letter has not been found). This brought a response dated 10th July, (the speed of mail delivery is astonishing!) stating that the R. and A. Secretary was in London but 'your letter will have immediate attention on his return'.

The R. and A. replies:

22nd July, 1936

The Secretary,
Ballater Golf Club
Dear Sir,

I refer to your letter of the 9th inst. and in reply I beg to state that Mr Anderson and Mr Young are disqualified for not returning their cards for the second round of the Summer Competition.

While the situation at the 7th Putting Green was most unfortunate the Committee of the Ballater Golf Club should not order the round to be replayed.

Yours faithfully,
Henry Gullen, Secretary

Mr Lemmon acknowledged the letter:

28th July, 1936

Many thanks for your letter of the 22nd July which I placed before the Golf Committee.

Your letter justifies the decision which the Committee had in mind, and the confirmation has been notified to the players concerned.

And wrote to Messrs Young and Anderson:

I have received from the Secretary of the St Andrews Club a reply in connection with your complaint of the 8th July.

In his letter he states that you are both disqualified for not returning your cards after the round of golf and instructing the Ballater Golf Committee not to order the round to be replayed.

Who responded by return:

29th July, 1936

The Secretary,
Ballater Golf Club

Dear Sir,

We have to acknowledge receipt of your letter of 28th inst. which is not a reply to our complaint.

The cardinal point at issue viz: 'Sticking the flag into the Green and thereby deceiving us as to the direction of the hole' has been entirely evaded in your letter. . . . We presume reference was made to this point by

151

the R and A Golf Club in their letter to you and we shall be glad to hear what they have to say on the subject.

With regard to the last paragraph of your letter we would point out that our cards were returned and accepted by you *without any comment as to disqualification*. We were also permitted to complete the two succeeding rounds the scores of which were accepted, *again without any comment as to disqualification*.

If it was intended by the Committee that we should be disqualified on these grounds we shall be glad of an explanation as to why we were not informed prior to commencing play in the 3rd round. A matter such as the return of a score card needs no reference to St Andrews when it is already laid down in the Rules of Golf.

We now await your Committee's explanations as to the points raised.

The Secretary replied that their letter would be placed in front of the Committee when it next met. No further reference to the matter can be found in the Club records. An inspection of the scores shows that I. Findlay playing off a handicap of 6 won the competition with a net score of 287 but playing off 8 Mr W.G.M. Anderson would have won with a second round of net 74. Alas the scores recorded on the disqualified cards are not revealed.

*   *   *

WRONG DAY

At a committee meeting on 24th September 1906 the following letter was read:

You are aware that a semi-final for the Club's medal was arranged to be played today. We the undersigned played our match on that date with following result: Thomson 89, Proctor 94. We have learned, however, that the other two competitors, Messrs Smart and Willox played their match on the 18th [i.e. the day before]. This seems to us to be a direct breach of all the rules of golf and we therefore protest against the result of their match being accepted by the Committee as valid.

We trust that you will bring this matter before the Committee and we shall be obliged if you will favour us with their findings.

N.J. Thomson   John Proctor

The committee found against Messrs Smart and Willox and they were disqualified.

152

NINETEEN

The Ballater Caddies

It was in the middle of the month o' June
And the weather was rotten in Ballater Toon
And the Ballater caddies renowned far and wide
began to look big and put on a bit side.
They werna contented, the pey was ower sma'
They wanted a shilling but that wisna a'
They got up a petition and ilka ane signed
Ane said to the ither weel get it you'll find.
However the days and the weeks flew away
The season wore on still na word of mair pay.
Till ilka ane grumalt and each said the like
'if they dinna give in we'el a' ging on strike'.
But one wise apostle named Philip the Wise
(This chappies richt fat, he's ower fond of his pies)
He said it's nae eese lads, they winna give in,
Though we a' ging on strike they'll na care a pin.
Your richt enough Jimmy, the maist o' them said
The gents noo-a-days think we're well enough paid.
So a' then agreed to give it a rest
They still work for a 'tanner' and hope for the best.

Peter (Spike) Davidson.

Rothimay, Ballater, 1907

    At a meeting on 11th May 1906 it was agreed to fix the charge for Caddies at 1/1 per round, the 1d to be retained by the Club. But then there were second thoughts when, next month Mr Smart proposed and Mr Jebb seconded that caddy charges be reduced from 1/1 to 8p a round—6p to the caddy and 2p to the club. This led to some unrest but it wasn't until August 1911 that John Hanna, the Ranger, informed a meeting:

> that the boys refused to caddie that morning unless they received 1/- per round and were only persuaded to go back to their work by him offering to bring the matter before the general committee. The meeting unanimously agreed that the charge for a caddie remain as at present 8 pence per round. Boys refusing to accept this ruling to be sent off the course.

However a year later the committee relented and the caddie charge became 1/- again and caddies over the age of 16 were not to be engaged. In 1920 the charge became 1/6.

Ian Wright, a nephew of Paddy Porter, used to visit Ballater frequently (and still does) at holiday time in the thirties, and he recalls the times when the caddies would disappear when the Yarrow family appeared because of their practice of paying only 1/- for the round whereas the going rate was 1/6. However the Yarrows made up for it by throwing end of season parties at Monaltrie House for all the caddies.

TWENTY

The Club Licence

In 1953 only the Invercauld Hotel and the Station Restaurant held drink licenses. The Bar at the Station Restaurant closed half an hour after the arrival of the last train (8.30 p.m. on Sundays).

After an evening round in the Summer there was always a great rush to the Tinks bar at the Invercauld. The Club now saw a way to improve this situation.

At the A.G.M. in March 1953 Captain Frai proposed, seconded by Mr Ben Adam, that the new committee be instructed to explore the matter of obtaining a Licence for the Clubhouse. This was agreed unanimously. The Secretary wrote to the Factor and at a meeting held in July it was announced that a reply had been received intimating Captain Farquharson's refusal to give his consent to an application for a Licence. The committee decided to seek legal advice from the Town Clerk, Mr Alan Watt of Gray and Kellas, Solicitors asking him to obtain a copy of the Lease from the Factor.

In October 1953 Mr Watt wrote to the Club suggesting that before matters were taken further it would be as well to ascertain that a majority of the members were in favour of the premises being licenced. It was therefore decided to call an E.G.M., all members to be notified that the business of the meeting was 'To consider a Club Licence'.

The meeting was held in the Albert Memorial Hall on Monday 2nd November 1953. There were 32 members present including the Vice-Captain Mr A.J. Todd who was in the chair. Apologies were received from nineteen members. Following an explanation of the position as it stood, Ballater Schoolteacher D.E. Smith proposed:

> that the Committee of the Ballater Golf Club be empowered to take all necessary and reasonable steps to secure a licence for the Club at the

earliest possible date. This was seconded by Mr Michie. After some discussion Mr W.J. Fraser put forward an amendment 'that the application for a licence is unnecessary and uncalled for'. The amendment was seconded by Mr A.W. (Paddy) Logan, of the Invercauld Arms (!). The amendment was defeated by 21 votes to 6 and the motion carried. The chairman then announced that of the members who had apologised for absence 18 had signified their approval of the motion.

The position of the Club was discussed with the Town Clerk who later replied that the proposal had been put to the Town Council which had approved it in principle.

Alan Watt was invited to attend a meeting on 1st February 1954 to discuss the next move. Watt had had a meeting with the Factor who confirmed Captain Farquharson's position. It was now agreed that he would approach the Factor and suggest that the Laird meet a deputation from the Golf Club. In this event the Club would be represented by Dr Moir, Mr Hay, and D.E. Smith along with Mr Watt who would put the case.

Watt attended another meeting in March when he reported that the deputation had been successful and that he had received a letter from the Factor, Mr Briggs, to the effect that Captain Farquharson, though not entirely in agreement with the Club applying for a licence, had decided not to raise objection should the Club make an application. Mr Watt said that new Rules for the Club would have to be drawn up and he had prepared a draft from the Rules of other licenced Golf Clubs. The meeting also agreed to give the Secretary power to appoint a Chartered Accountant to audit the books in place of the two members who had been appointed at the last A.G.M. Gray and Kellas were appointed.

Gray and Kellas now required signatures for the Certificate as to the 'bona fides' of the Club. From the list of names of the Licensing Court for the Deeside District of Aberdeenshire the following were to be approached by Mr Watt: Colonel A.E. Stewart, Glengarden, Ballater and Mr James Smith, Bank House, Torphins.

On Sunday 9th May 1954 the Captain, Dr Moir, announced that the Club had been successful in obtaining the Licence, and the meeting turned its attention to the clubhouse alterations which would be required.

*   *   *

A.C.R. Watt, who died in 1989, was a distinguished scholar, soldier, and lawyer. His appointment as Town Clerk of Ballater brought him into close contact with the Club for almost twenty years until he resigned his partnership with Gray and Kellas in 1971 in order to take up the appointment as Chairman of Industrial Tribunals. When he retired in 1987 he was the most senior tribunal chairman in Scotland.

Alan Watt was of great assistance to the Club, intervening with the Laird at the time assistance was required in obtaining the Licence and when it was negotiating the purchase of the course. He did an enormous amount of work for the Club and for Ballater.

A.C.R. Watt

TWENTY ONE

Natural History Notes

BY GRAHAM MACDONALD OF THE BALLATER FIELD
CENTRE

Ballater—a small village some 40 miles west of Aberdeen and the only planned settlement in Royal Deeside—is set amongst some of the finest scenery in Scotland. The village and golf club sit on the bottom of the Dee valley, a valley carved by an enormous Glacier as it ground its way from the high Cairngorms to the North Sea. It is overlooked by the steep cliffs of Craigendarroch (Hill of Oaks) to the North and to the South by the tree clad slopes of Craig Coillich (Old Woman's Hill). To the West, a large meander of the river Dee provides a further physical barrier to the developement of this regal settlement. These features in turn give way to the far more impressive backdrop of the Coyles of Muick and that most majestic of all mountains—Lochnagar.

Eight miles west of Ballater is Balmoral Castle the summer retreat of Royalty since 1854, when Queen Victoria and Prince Albert purchased it from the Gordon family for the bargain price of £31,500.

Undoubtedly, this Royal association has much to do with the popularity the area enjoys with tourists, but of equal importance must surely be the unrivalled scenery where mountain stream, tree clad slopes and and rocky crag fill every vista.

If the area in general enjoys unsurpassed scenery, then the golf course must also be amongst the most breathtaking in the country. Indeed those playing on Ballater's greens and fairways are treated not only to a marvellous golf course but to some stunning scenery and glimpses of a whole range of flora and fauna; to evidence of the changing nature of the landscape, and the role that the river played in shaping not only this golf course but some of the surrounding landscape.

It would be difficult to attempt to describe, in any systematic way, the natural history interest of the golf course, so varied and so seasonal is it.

Indeed regular golfers must themselves see the course change with the seasons, each season competing with the previous for aesthetic prominence. Some features, the river, Craigendarroch Hill, the splendid view of Lochnagar from the 16th fairway are to be seen throughout the seasons, albeit in ever changing livery. Others, like the soaring buzzards or the autumnal oaks of Craigendarroch are but transient features in an ever changing landscape.

Without exception each tee, green and fairway has something different to offer, but the first fairway is, perhaps, the best, offering as it does splendid vistas to all points of the compass. There is an amazing variety of plant life on the edges of the fairways and in the light rough. Unfortunately, the close cutting regime of the ground staff makes it very difficult to identify them. However, the vibrant yellow of the broom and the gorse is a significant feature of the course in early summer as is the blue haze of scabious and harebell in mid summer. Significantly, the exposed nature of the course leads to extremely windy conditions in some parts, and this is reflected in the wind-blasted shape of the trees particularly on the fifth fairway, which was almost certainly the bed of the river before it meandered farther across the valley bottom. In fact much of the ground on which the golf course stands was once a river-bed.

Despite the abundance of trees to be seen in the distance, there are surprisingly few on the course itself, and it is not until the 11th tee and the area beside the river that we get near to what one might call a sylvan setting, with the wonderful sounds of the small woodland birds who make their homes in these majestic Scots Pines. Even here the vegetation is not left to flourish unhindered—there is much evidence of browsing animals, particularly hares, the bark on the smaller trees having been removed for food during the harsh Ballater winters. On the subject of trees, the 14th green is overlooked by a stand of Aspen. These trees provide one of the finest sights on the course, their leaves dancing ever so gracefully in even the lightest of breezes.

One of the attractions of Ballater is its climate, and in particularly the number of clear, sunny days. From the 15th fairway we can see one of the many houses in Ballater which takes advantage of this, and has installed solar collectors on the roof to help offset the high winter heating costs. This house not only exploits its southerly aspect to steal energy from the sun but it also enjoys magnificent views south to The Coyles and beyond to Lochnagar—views which typify the natural beauty of this outstanding golf course.

The undermentioned species may be seen on or from the golf course. The list is not, of course, exhaustive.

It is unlikely that many mammals will be seen during a round of golf but there is ample evidence of the following:

hares   droppings and browsing
rabbits   droppings
roe deer   browsing
squirrels   eaten cones

Birds

Black Headed Gull
Blackbird
Blue Tit
Buzzard
Chaffinch
Coal Tit
Collared Dove
Crow
Curlew
Dipper
Heron
Fieldfare

Geese
Great Tit
Greenfinch
House Martin
Jackdaw
Kestrel
Long Tailed Tit
Mallard
Meadow Pipit
Osprey
Oyster Catcher
Pied Wagtail

Redwing
Robin
Sand Martin
Siskin
Sparrow
Starling
Swallow
Swift
Thrush — Mistle
  and Song
Wood Pigeon

Wild Flowers

Anemone
Bistort
Broom
Bugle
Clover
Cow Parsley
Dog Violet
Foxglove

Gorse
Harebell
Heath Bedstraw
Milkwort
Nettle
Nootka Lupin
Plantain
Primrose

Purple Vetch
Rose Bay
Willow Herb
Scabious
Speedwell
Stitchwort
Tormentil
Wood

Trees

Alder
Aspen
Cypress
Douglas Fir
Norway Spruce
Oak

Rowan
Scots Pine
Silver Birch
Whitebeam
Willow

160

TWENTY TWO

The Seniors

The Ballater Golf Club Seniors' Section (entry at 55) was formed in 1990, later than most of the down-river neighbouring clubs where active senior sections were already organising inter-club matches and home course activities. The prime mover behind the formation of the Section was A.R. Clark, former Edinburgh Civil Servant, Ballater Hotelier, and enthusiastic golfer (and fisher). It was right and proper when the Club Council agreed in 1989 that the section should be formed, that Alex Clark should be its first co-ordinator. Walter MacLennan and Jimmy Stewart (both with Veterinary connections) were elected to join Alex on the small committee.

At the Seniors A.G.M. in October 1991 Dr Peter Crawford was elected co-ordinator.

In its first full season (1990) the section played home and away matches against Aboyne, Banchory and Royal Aberdeen. In 1991 the match programme included these clubs plus Deeside and Duff House Royal.

The matches vary in numbers from eight to sixteen players, or as many as can be raised up to say twenty for Ballater—Royal Aberdeen has about 75 Seniors which results in a rationing of match activity. There is no such problem at Ballater where most active Seniors can play in most matches.

The match formats are designed to create a social atmosphere with lunch or refreshments included and subsidised by benevolent Club Councils. Maureen Todd plays a large part in the success of the Seniors because the quality of the food that she prepares and serves is unmatched on Deeside.

*   *   *

161

Seniors at work. Top left: Walter MacLennan (with tie) keeps an eye on A.R. Clark who appears to be adjusting the scores. Bill Jarvis stands over Sandy Thomson. Bottom left: John MacLeman makes a point to Don Culling and Ira Slater (with pipe). Centre: A.R. Clark. Top right: Maureen Todd with customers Jim Crawford (left) and Sandy Grant. Front foreground is Ian Cruickshank. Bottom right: Norman Thain addresses Ian Cruickshank.

The final match in the 1991 season was played against Royal Aberdeen at Balgownie on September 12th. It was sad that the night before the game, burglars had stolen the Aberdeen Club's valuable collection of old clubs and balls, but from the Ballater point of view the match was a great success—a half at Balgownie seems like a win! The teams on the day were:

Royal Aberdeen		Ballater
R. Mackinnon+B. Petrie	halved	with W. Manson+D. Culling
J. Finnie+S. Clark	lost to	A. Grant+A. Clark
D. Patterson+I. Robb	lost to	N. Thain+D. Joss
A. Nicholson+R. Gallon	beat	A. Ingram+P. MacPhee
G. MacKinnon+J. Hay	lost to	W. MacLennan+W. Lawson
J. Davidson+W. Robinson	beat	I. Slater+E. Reid
J. Ruddiman+J. Innes	beat	J. Beaton+C. Puddicombe
R. Ellis+G. Smith	lost to	M. Michie+H. Wright
K. Laing+W. Brown	beat	A. Mutch+P. Crawford

Match result: four all with one halved.

163

APPENDIX ONE

List of Patrons in 1905

At the Annual Meeting of the Golf Club held on 3rd May 1905 it was decided to ask the following ladies and gentlemen to become Patrons:

Captain and Mrs A.H. Farquharson of Invercauld
Sir Allan and Lady MacKenzie of Glen Muick

> MacKenzie was born in 1850 and he died 20th August 1906. He married Lucy, daughter of Duncan Davidson of Tullich. He built the huge Glen Muick House (it had 365 windows!) which was pulled down after the last war when it had suffered greatly at the hands of billeted troops. Brackley House, nearby, became Glen Muick House and is now owned by Sir Peter Walker-Okeover.

H.G. Anderson Esq., Park House, Wimbledon, London, and Oakhall, Ballater
F.J. Yarrow Esq., Newton, Ballater
Rudolphe Christen Esq., St. Imier, Bridge o' Gairn

> Artist. Born at St Imier, Canton Berne, Switzerland on 26th April, 1859. He died at St Imier, Brig o' Gairn, Ballater on 7th September 1906. St Imier is now the McEwan Gallery

Alexander Keiller Esq., Craigendarroch
Dr George Ogilvie, Edinburgh
Dr Joseph Ogilvie, Church of Scotland Training College, Aberdeen
H.S.F. Jebb Esq. Tullich Lodge
Reginald Gordon Esq., of Abergeldie
Colonel Gordon, Bydand, Ballater
Colonel Boyce, Mount Stewart, Ballater
Andrew Smith, Esq., Estate Office, Invercauld
G.B. Pasley Esq., Highland Home, Ballater
John Michie Esq., Abergeldie Mains, Balmoral

T. Jameson Torry Esq. Monaltrie
Misses Mackieson and Judkin, 33 Upper Addison Gardens, London
Mrs Hayne, St Ronans, Aberdeen, and Beauvais, Ballater
Miss Westby, Ravenswood, Ballater, and Albert Hall Mansions, Kensington Gore, London, S.W.

The list of Patrons for the Bazaar in 1907 was much the same as the Golf Club Patrons in 1905 but there were additions:
Her Royal Highness the Duchess of Connaught
Their Excellencies the Earl and Countess of Aberdeen
Lord and Lady Kilmarnock, 3 Reisner Strasse 19, Vienna

> Lord Kilmarnock married Mary Lucy Victoria daughter of Sir Allan MacKenzie of Glen Muick. He was in the Diplomatic Corps.

Sir John Forbes Clark, Bart. of Tillypronnie

> Career Diplomat. Son of Sir James Clark, Physician to Queen Victoria. He married Charlotte daughter of Hon. Sir Thomas J. Coltman, a Justice of the Queen's Bench, of Blelack.

Sir Victor MacKenzie, Bart of Glenmuick
Right Hon. Robert Farquharson of Finzean

> M.P. for West Aberdeenshire 1880 to 1906.

Mr and Mrs Barclay-Harvey of Dinnet
Mr and Mrs J.F. Gaskell of Cambus o' May

> John Francis Gaskell lived in Cambus O' May House (now a Hotel). He died in 1910. Gaskell made considerable contributions to the cost of construction of the present St Kentigern's Church and its Rectory on Braemar Road known as Glenshiel. Mrs Gaskell gifted the Clergy Stalls carved by James Ogilvie and Sons of Aberdeen.

Mr and Mrs W.H. Coltman of Deskrie

> Mr Coltman inherited most of Tillypronie Estate on death of Sir John Clark in 1910.

Mr and Mrs Neuman, Glenmuick.
Mr Crewdson, Gairnsheil
Mr J.M. Henderson, M.P. and Mrs Henderson
Mr and Mrs John Rennie, Glenbardie
The Misses Farquharson, Tigh-na-Roid, Braemar
Miss Farquharson, London
Mrs Fenwick and the Misses Fenwick, Adbury House, Newbury
Mrs Tocher, London

APPENDIX TWO

Braid/Vardon Luncheon Invitations

16TH AUGUST, 1906

Acceptances:

Dr A.C. Profeit

Dr Alexander Hendry of Netherly, Ballater. Dr Hendry purchased Darroch Learg from J.T.B. Alexander in 1909.

H.S.F. Jebb, Tullich Lodge, Ballater

D. Wilkie, Melrose, Queens Road, Ballater

The Rev. S.J. Ramsay Sibbald, The Manse, Crathie, N.B.

Henry Illingworth Esq., Balgairn

Mr J. Barclay Rennett, 231a Union St. Aberdeen

Colonel Gordon, Bydand, Ballater

Francis T. Maddock Esq., Bheinn-Raineach, Ballater

Colonel Boyce, Mount Stewart, Ballater

J.F. Gaskell Esq., of Cambus o' May House

Mr Middleton, Heatherbank

Mr Victor MacKenzie, Brackley, Ballater

Lord Kilmarnock, Brackley, Ballater

The Rev. J.H. Burn, Ballater

A.H. Farquharson Esq., Invercauld Arms Hotel, Braemar

John McGregor Esq., Braemar

Alex McHardy Esq., Dorsincilly, Ballater

Mr Henry Kellas, 48 Carden Place, Aberdeen

Mr C.C. Smith, (Aboyne Golf Club), Post Office, Aboyne

William W. Tytler Esq., The Cottage, Ballater

William Beekie Esq., Golf Road, Ballater

The Rev. E.N. Sharpe, Valetta Villa, Ballater

James D. Brebner Esq., Aboyne
Donald Gordon, Deeside Hydropathic, (now Tor na Dee) Murtle
Mr Littlejohn, Osborne House, Ballater
P. Grant Esq., The Towers, Ballater
John Smith Esq., Oakleigh, Ballater
Major General Stileman, Glen Lui, Ballater
Mr John Simpson, Union Bank House, Ballater
Mr MacDonald, Fife Arms Hotel, Braemar
Mr Sandison, Huntley Arms Hotel, Aboyne
W. Smith Esq., Altdouray, Ballater
Mr King, Craigneuk, Ballater
James Williams Esq., Dakolei, Aboyne
Reginald H.L. Gordon Esq., Clachanturn, Abergeldie
William Duguid, J.P., Deebank House, Ballater
Mr Alfred William Edwards, Justice of Peace Clerk's Office, 29 Union
St., Aberdeen.
John Lawson, Schoolhouse, Ballater
Robert Williams Esq., Craiglarach, Aboyne
Donald Munro Esq., Ravenswood
John Smart. Deeside Railway & Carting Contractor

Regrets:
Sir Allan MacKenzie, Brackley, Ballater

A letter witten by his daughter, Lucy Kilmarnock, conveys Sir Allan's
regret that he is too ill to attend and suggests that, if the Club wished,
either his son Victor or Lord Kilmarnock 'would be very glad to come to
your help'.

Alexander Mitchell, Sluievannachie, Ballater
Rudolphe Christen, St Imier, Brig o' Gairn, Ballater

The letter was written by Christen's wife Sydney who enclosed a cheque
for £1–1–0 at his request. Christen was ill and he died the following
month.

Mr M.M. Duncan, Royal Aberdeen Golf Club
Mr G.B. Pasley, Highland Home, Ballater
Mr John Rennie, Glenbardie, Ballater
Mr Barclay-Harvey, Dinnet R.S.O. Aberdeenshire
William Brown, Braemar
Mr Tom Lambert, East View, Silsden, West Riding, Yorkshire
Dr A.R. Laing, Pathology Dept., Marischal College, Aberdeen
Mr Knox, Milton of Tullich, Ballater
John Littlejohn Esq., The Haugh, Cambus o' May
Mr F. Coutts, Town & County Bank Ltd,. Ballater

APPENDIX THREE

The Man who Pitched for Success — with Tent Pegs

BY JOHN CAMPBELL

The success of 27 year-old Walker Cup player Sandy Pirie, head green-keeper at Hazlehead, in the recent [1970] Northern Open championship at Cruden Bay on the battered north eastern coastline of Aberdeen was the first by an amateur for 34 years and was something I thought I might never see again.

In diabolical weather which included a blizzard of North Pole intensity that deposited two inches of snow on the course in a period of ten minutes, Pirie's performance against a top class professional field that included a number of Ryder Cup players speaks for itself.

So it is not of this year's winner that I wish to speak, but rather of the last amateur to accomplish the feat, a strange, handsome young Adonis whose first round of golf was a 72 (he practised for a year before going on to the course) and who became a legend in his own lifetime.

Up north, where so many of their men wrest a living from the cruel North Sea, seemingly hewn from the native granite and without the fisherman's penchant for tall stories, they speak of Dick Walker of Aberdeen University with an awe which comes so close to disbelief that one is left with the feeling that he may have been a visitor from another planet.

That he was very real indeed I can vouch for personally and so can a few of my friends.

In these far off days there was a regular northern circuit of holiday tournaments and I had heard tales of the prowess of this strange young man who hitch-hiked round the north, carrying with only a little white tent which he pitched as close as possible to the practice ground and a large black leather golf bag which contained his toilet requisites in the ball pocket.

He wore only a sailor's rough blue jersey, shorts, and a pair of sandshoes.

My first sight of him was at Dornoch, in 1935, when he won the first of his two successive Northern Opens.

When I looked out of my bedroom window in the early morning I was amazed to see a man standing on one leg, completely motionless like a giant seagull on top of a fencing post.

He was still there when I finished breakfast and when asked what he thought he was doing he replied that he was adjusting his balance for the day, and an involved explanation of the importance of the middle ear in playing good golf.

My own preparation of swinging a driver a few times and snatching a couple of practice putts seemed rather sketchy by contrast, and the more so by comparison of our two cards at the end of the day.

This feeling of inadequacy was shared by my friend, Donald Cameron, a Scottish international who tells a lovely story of encountering Dick Walker in the entrance hall of the Clubhouse before their meeting in the Scottish championship.

Walker's large bag contained a small pencil bag and as they conversed for a few moments Cameron became aware that he was under close scrutiny.

One wooden club, a putter and five irons were transferred to the pencil bag and Walker toyed briefly with his driver before pushing it firmly back into the bag and deciding he would not require it. An additional medium iron got the same consideration before it too was discarded.

As the outraged Donald Cameron tells the story he leaves the listener in no doubt that young Walker would pay dearly for his arrogance.

'And what was the result?' I remember asking. 'Seven and six and a long walk back,' said Cameron with feigned relish.

The story is the better, of course, in that the large margin was in Walker's favour!

Cameron should probably have felt honoured in that Walker rated him as value for seven clubs—other opponents had commanded no more than five.

Among other peculiarities, Dick Walker was the first person I ever heard of who 'marked his card' in the manner of the modern Americans.

At the start of a round he informed his opponent that he preferred not to talk. His paces were a full yard and he subtracted the total from the yardage on the card, thereby selecting his club for the next stroke.

169

He hit the ball straighter than anyone I have ever seen except perhaps the great Jack McLean.

He vanished from the north as unobstrusively as he had arrived and where he is now no one knows. Perhaps he went to America and started them all on 'casing' the course during their practice rounds, noting the distance of various hazards and landmarks from tee to green.

One thing is certain. Whatever else he may have been he was assuredly what the modern assembly line dismally fails to produce—a 'character'.

[R.S. (Dick) Walker died on 16th January 1992.]

APPENDIX FOUR

The Ternemny Farm Ogilvies

Dr George Ogilvie was born around 1830 at Ternemny Farm, Rothiemay, the second of six brothers:

William	Rector, Milne's Institution, Fochabers
George	Rector, George Watson's College, Edinburgh
Alexander	Headmaster Robert Gordon's College, Aberdeen
Joseph	Rector, Church of Scotland Training College, Aberdeen
Robert	Chief Inspector of Schools, Scotand
James	Farmed at Rothiemay

170

APPENDIX FIVE

Ballater Shops in 1906

R.W. Abel. Painter and Decorator, Victoria Road.

Alexander Anderson. Baker and Confectioner, Church Square.

William Barnett. General Stores, Groceries, Provisions, Ironmongery, Drapery and Haberdashery.

J. & J. Bisset, Ballater and Aboyne. Photography.

George Cook & Co., Plumbers, Sanitary Engineers, Electric Bell Fitters & Tinsmiths. Deebank Road.

Thomas Cowie, Bridge Street. Family Grocer and Draper. Golfing Suits and Costumes a speciality.

Alexander Craig. General Merchant. Provisions. Harris's Wiltshire Bacon. Choice Danish and Finest Home Butter and Eggs from the Farm daily. Lowest Possible Prices.

Davidson's Cash Stores, Bridge Street. Tailoring Department, Braemar Road ... Wincey and Grandrill Shirts, Lambs Wool, Merino, and Cashmere underclothing. Ready-made knicker hose, Backcombs, Side combs etc.

William Duguid & Son. Painters, Glaziers, Paper Hangers, Builders, and Valuators.

William Duguid. Carpenter, Joiner, Glazier, Cartwright and Undertaker. Shop: Victoria Road. House: Church Square.

John Findlay, Bridge Street. Practical Taxidermist. Golfing Requisites, Agent for Archibald's Clubs.

James Grant. Slater and Cement Worker.

Grant Brothers. Builders

James Halket, Bridge Street. Chemist. (from Davidson & Kay, Chemists to the King, Aberdeen, and Hitchock & Co. Oxford), Physicians Prescriptions.

J. Knowles & Son, Bridge Street. Practical Watch and Clockmakers,

Jewellers, Opticians, Engravers etc.

John Leith & Son, Bridge Street. Bread and Biscuit Bakers and Confectioners ... beg to intimate to the Visitors that they use the choicest Danish Butter only ...

James McGregor. Draper, Grocer, General Merchant, Bridge Street.

A. MacKenzie. Bookseller, Picture Postcards, All the Principal Newspapers, Periodicals delivered daily immediately on arrival of trains. Circulating Library.

John Malcolm & Co. Bakery. Tea Room.

Misses Michie, Glenaden, Ballater. Three Public Rooms, one Parlour, Nine Bedrooms, one Servants' Room, Bathroom, H. and C. Kitchen, Scullery, Cycle-room, Garden etc.

John Milne, Ballater and Braemar. Carting Agent. Luggage and Parcels Delivery. Hay, Oats, Straw etc.

William Milne, Braemar and Ballater. Bootmaker.

John Mitchell. Saddler and Harness Maker.

Mrs Murray. Grocer, Golf Road.

William Robb. Jeweller, Ballater, Braemar.

Simpsons for High Class foot-wear. Golfing Boots and Shoes.

John Smith. Builder, Slater, and Sanitary Engineer, Ballater.

William W. Tytler, Bridge Street. Dispensing and Family Chemist.

Alexander Troup. Purveyor of Meat, Poulterer and Greengrocer.

William Whyte, (successor to Francis Coutts), Station Square, Ballater. Drapery, Ironmongery, Grocery. Agent for Bon-Accord Steam Laundry.

David Wilkie, Gents and boys Outfitter. Highland Costumes, Harris and Donegal Tweeds.

William Willox. Cycle Agent, Braemar Road and Bridge Street.

172

APPENDIX SIX

Programme for Centenary Week—1st to 9th August 1992

Saturday	1st August	Annual 36 hole Open
Sunday	2nd ,,	Mixed foursomes. Supper/Dance
Monday	3rd ,,	Ladies Day. Dinner at 9 p.m.
Tuesday	4th ,,	Mens Day. Supper at 9 p.m.
Wednesday	5th ,,	Centenary Day. Dinner at 8 p.m.
Thursday	6th ,,	Seniors Day. High Tea at 8 p.m.
Friday	7th ,,	Juniors Day. Disco.
Saturday	8th ,,	Ladies 18 hole Open.
Sunday	9th ,,	Mixed Stableford. 8 p.m. Prizes/Supper.

OTHER IMPORTANT GOLFING EVENTS IN 1992

May 9th to 15th	Royal Deeside Golf Week
May 29th to 31st	Aberdeenshire County Ladies Championship
June 6th to 13th	The Society of One-Armed golfers—Championships
July 27th to 30th	Scottish Veteran Ladies Championship
August 15th and 16th	North-east District Mens 72 hole Open

173

Index

Note: This index does not include names listed in Appendices One, Two or Five

174